# THE ZODIAC PATH

## Align Your Life with the Stars

ARIES
TAURUS
PISCES
GEMINI
AQUARIUS
CANCER
CAPRICORN
LEO
SAGITTARIUS
VIRGO
SCORPIO
LIBRA

Publications International, Ltd.

**Jill M. Phillips** has authored of dozens of books and hundreds of articles on astrology. She regularly wrote forecast columns for *Astrology: Your Daily Horoscope* and has contributed to *Globe*'s mini-magazine astrology series.

Images from Shutterstock.com

Louis Weber, CEO
Publications International, Ltd.
8140 Lehigh Avenue
Morton Grove, IL 60053

ISBN: 978-1-63938-100-5

Manufactured in China.

8 7 6 5 4 3 2 1

**Let's get social!**
 @Publications_International
 @PublicationsInternational
**www.pilbooks.com**

# CONTENTS

# INTRODUCTION

The study of astrology—the prediction of personality traits and the divination of future events based on the relationship between the sun, moon, and planets—dates back thousands of years, to the ancient Egyptians, who were the first to make a science of it. The Babylonians, Greeks, and Romans also held it in high esteem.

Today, astrology is hugely popular. And thanks to the personal computer, astrologers can cast and interpret a chart in minutes—work that in the past would have taken weeks.

## SUN SIGN ASTROLOGY

Sun sign astrology is the study of the twelve signs of the zodiac. Each of us fits into one of these twelve categories. (See the sun sign birth chart on page 7.) You don't need to have your chart analyzed to discover a great deal about your natal (at-birth) characteristics or to get an idea of influences at work in your life.

# ELEMENTS AND NATURE

The twelve sun signs are divided into elements: Fire, Earth, Air, Water. The elements help to describe the basic nature of a sign. For example, Fire signs (Aries, Leo, Sagittarius) have "firelike" characteristics: a hot temper, passion, creativity, and boldness. Earth signs (Taurus, Virgo, Capricorn) are stable, frugal, and sensual. People born under Air signs (Gemini, Libra, Aquarius) are intellectually inclined, changeable, and high-strung. Water-sign people (Cancer, Scorpio, Pisces) are intuitive, spiritual, and secretive.

# USING THIS BOOK

*The Zodiac Path* is a carefully researched guide intended for use by the general public. Whether your interest in astrology is new or of long-standing, you'll find this book useful, fascinating, and fun. Each chapter begins with an intriguing overview of a sun sign, followed by an advice-filled profile for each birth date that falls within that sun sign.

Your birth date is special because it is yours. Use *The Zodiac Path* as a small step on your path to understanding all that you are, and everything you have to offer.

# HOW WE DID IT

The exclusive insights you'll find in *The Zodiac Path* are based upon a variety of methods designed to analyze days within each sun sign. First, a careful examination was made of the traits and personality characteristics of the sun sign itself, as well as the myriad associations related to its planetary ruler. Further division and definition of each sign were provided by the use of dwads (2.5-degree markers) and decanates (10-degree markers), which establish an even more specific profile.

Finally, numerology (the study of the divine and magical significance of numbers) and use of the Sabian symbols (a set of 360-degree symbols that describe arcane and modern symbology) were utilized to attain even greater definition and accuracy.

| | |
|---|---|
| Aries • March 21–April 20 | Libra • September 23–October 22 |
| Taurus • April 21–May 20 | Scorpio • October 23–November 21 |
| Gemini • May 21–June 20 | Sagittarius • November 22–December 21 |
| Cancer • June 21–July 22 | Capricorn • December 22–January 19 |
| Leo • July 23–August 22 | Aquarius • January 20–February 18 |
| Virgo • August 23–September 22 | Pisces • February 19–March 20 |

# SUN SIGN BIRTH CHART

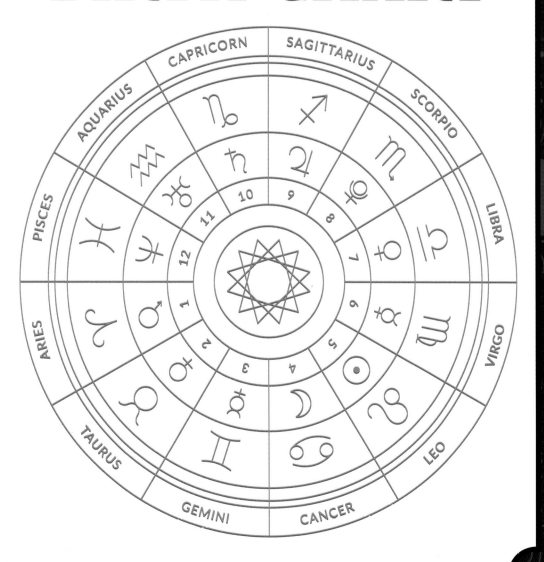

# ARIES

## March 21–April 20

Aries is the first sign of the astrological year and known by its astrological symbol, the Ram. Aries individuals are willful, positive, and independent. With Mars as the ruling planet, people born under this sign are thought to be warlike and aggressive. They have amazing stamina and a potent drive to succeed.

**Element:** Fire
**Planetary ruler:** Mars
**Key characteristic:** Leadership
**Strengths:** Intelligent; assertive; adventurous
**Challenges:** Trouble with sharing; too much ego; vindictive

# March 21 • Aries

You have a proud, adventuresome, and energetic nature, though this may not be displayed in conventional ways. You are sure of yourself and your convictions, but you may fear being ridiculed for your great dreams. For this reason you are likely to adopt a "who cares" attitude, when in truth you care very much. You have incredible emotional resilience and can easily bounce back from disappointment. You have a quiet intensity that is riveting. Although you do not make a great display of yourself, you draw others to you easily. Positions of power come naturally to March 21 individuals, whether in the business or academic arenas.

**Embrace:** Good intentions; hard work; satisfaction in a job well done

**Avoid:** Superstition; indolence; becoming too cautious

**Also born on this day:** Actors Matthew Broderick and Gary Oldman; poet Phyllis McGinley; auto racer Ayrton Senna; theatrical producer Florenz Ziegfeld

# March 22 • Aries

Instinct takes precedence over intellect in your life. You are impulsive and fun-loving. You enjoy testing boundaries and breaking the rules. You are vibrant and exciting and can draw people to you on the strength of your personality alone. You are a natural leader, but not in the conventional sense. Others envy your love of daring and risk-taking. You have the highest expectations for your own success and may be unable to recognize the pitfalls that are possible when striving hard to reach a goal. A strong belief in yourself is a key factor in your overall success.

**Embrace:** Quiet reflection; doing good deeds; accentuating the positive

**Avoid:** Personal obsessions; needless worry; bad habits

**Also born on this day:** Mime Marcel Marceau; author James Patterson; actors William Shatner and Reese Witherspoon; composer/lyricist Stephen Sondheim; composer/producer Andrew Lloyd Webber

# March 23 • Aries

People born on this date are self-deprecating, good-natured folks who typically don't take themselves too seriously. You approach life with gusto and are never at a loss to find new and interesting subjects to engage your intellect. You have a quick mind and are able to store facts on many subjects for use at later times. Talkative and outgoing, you give the appearance of being highly organized, though you actually prefer to take life as it comes, favoring spontaneity over any carefully orchestrated plan to succeed. You have high expectations but leave it up to providence to make your dreams come true.

**Embrace:** Emotional depth; spiritual goals; destiny

**Avoid:** Excessive temperament; ignoring details; intolerance

**Also born on this day:** Musician Damon Albarn; rocket scientist Wernher von Braun; actors Joan Crawford and Catherine Keener; NBA guard Kyrie Irving; Eugenie, Princess of York; film director Akira Kurosawa

# March 24 • Aries

You are a creative, sympathetic type and see your life as an expression of your deep inner creativity. Your good nature extends to associations with everyone around you, and you are unlikely to have enemies. You possess a delightful naïveté that in no way implies a lack of intelligence or sophistication. You manage to combine these qualities with a simplicity that attracts admirers. You have a general idea of what you want to happen in your life, but it is likely to be tempered by your wonder and enjoyment at watching events unfold in your own time.

**Embrace:** Hard choices; spiritual harmony; patience

**Avoid:** Losing momentum; codependency; negative thoughts

**Also born on this day:** Bank robber Clyde Barrow; women's and civil rights activist Dorothy Height; magician Harry Houdini; quarterback Peyton Manning; actors Lara Flynn Boyle, Robert Carradine, Steve McQueen, and Jim Parsons

# March 25 • Aries

Your inner nature is very different from your outer personality. You have strong social skills and others may consider you the life of the party. But in reality you are naturally shy, preferring your own company to crowds. You draw strength from a rich and creative inner life. Although your love life is often turbulent, sometimes even tragic, romance is the focal point of your life. You may have many social friends, but very few close ones. There are few goals in life you cannot achieve once you put your mind to it.

**Embrace:** Positive outflow; emotional resonance; being young at heart

**Avoid:** Pessimism; looking back instead of forward; being sullen

**Also born on this day:** Agronomist/Nobel Prize laureate Norman Borlaug; singer Aretha Franklin; singer/songwriter Sir Elton John; novelist Flannery O'Connor; actor Sarah Jessica Parker; author/activist Gloria Steinem

# March 26 • Aries

On the surface you appear to be capable, even unflappable, yet there is a deep insecurity at your core that at times creates emotional distress. You are unlikely to show your vulnerabilities to the world. You prefer to handle your own challenges, solve your own problems. You believe in your own ability to make things happen, yet if something cannot be accomplished according to your own concepts of honesty and integrity, you would just as soon not see your goals come to fruition. Careers in productive, useful fields work best for people born on March 26.

**Embrace:** Displaying sensitivity; a sense of beauty; being happy

**Avoid:** Being secretive; ignoring the needs of others; sarcasm

**Also born on this day:** Poet Robert Frost; actors James Caan, Keira Knightley, and Leonard Nimoy; Supreme Court Justice Sandra Day O'Connor; House Speaker Nancy Pelosi; singer Diana Ross; playwright Tennessee Williams

# March 27 • Aries

Strength and tenacity are your defining characteristics. You generally go your own way and make your decisions according to your impulsive nature. At times this impulsiveness can be a drawback in your relationships with others, since it tends to make you seem bossy, even arrogant. In reality, nothing could be further from the truth. You dream big dreams and expect them to come true. You work amazingly hard to achieve these ends, never expecting good fortune to come easily.

**Embrace:** Teamwork; true love; lost causes

**Avoid:** Insincerity; becoming disillusioned; trying too hard

**Also born on this day:** Singers Mariah Carey and Fergie; actors Judy Carne, Gloria Swanson, and Michael York; filmmaker Quentin Tarantino

# March 28 • Aries

You have a bubbly, excitable, and somewhat unpredictable personality. You can be argumentative, but never to the point where it diminishes your great personal charm. At your core you are thoughtful, meditative, and spiritual. You spend a great deal of time and effort balancing these conflicting qualities. Even when you don't have a specific goal in mind, you are on a constant pilgrimage to improve your life. You invariably draw others into this personal commitment to excellence, inspiring them in ways no one else could.

**Embrace:** Opportunity; making good choices; honest emotion

**Avoid:** Putting yourself first; demanding perfection; being petty

**Also born on this day:** Singers Lady Gaga and Reba McEntire; Renaissance artist Raphael (Raffaello Sanzio); actor Vince Vaughn

# March 29 • Aries

There is a poetic quality to the people born on this day, a sense of combining the insubstantial with the ethereal. You have the ability to transcend the ordinary aspects of your personality by drawing upon a penetrating intelligence and extraordinary gifts of intuition. You do not always realize you are making a determination by instinct rather than intelligence. You are extra sensitive to the thoughts and projections of others and are incredibly connected to the people in your life. Friendship has a special meaning for you, and you wisely choose friends who are as different from yourself as possible.

**Embrace:** Treating others fairly; being generous; giving compliments

**Avoid:** Envy; wishing others ill; wasting time

**Also born on this day:** Singer Pearl Bailey; comedian Eric Idle; U.S. president John Tyler; Walmart founder Sam Walton; baseball legend Cy Young

# March 30 • Aries

You are renowned for your sense of humor. Bold and generous, you live life to the fullest and are seldom afraid to take chances on your self-appointed path to wisdom and enlightenment. You are an enthusiastic and dynamic individual with the ability to spur others to action. You make a fine mentor and will go to any lengths to help friends and associates attain their goals. You know what you want out of life. Even though you may end up taking a rather circuitous route to get where you are going, you have judgment enough to understand that sometimes the journey is more enlightening than the final destination.

**Embrace:** Poignant reminiscences; cheerfulness; your special talent

**Avoid:** Hurtful criticism; superficial friendships; personality conflicts

**Also born on this day:** Actor Warren Beatty; musician Eric Clapton; singers Celine Dion and Norah Jones; artist Vincent van Gogh

# March 31 • Aries

Your uniqueness owes itself in part to your ability to recognize unusual opportunities. You often seem to be in the path of miraculous good fortune, but it is to your credit that when such a rendezvous takes place, you know how to benefit from it. You have a great deal of charisma and can make things happen by the strength and force of your personality alone. You are ambitious about making your dreams become reality. You don't hold yourself to set standards, preferring to chart your own course. Far from being concerned with your own success, you like to feel that your choices influence and even benefit humankind.

**Embrace:** Synergy; faithfulness; confidence

**Avoid:** Senseless unpredictability; being late; self-doubt

**Also born on this day:** Composer Johann Sebastian Bach; activist Cesar Chavez; designer Liz Claiborne; philosopher René Descartes; U.S. vice president Al Gore; boxer Jack Johnson; actor Ewan McGregor

# April 1 • Aries

Despite your connection to this questionable "holiday," you are anything but a fool. You are a leader, though not in the conventional sense of that word. Your quiet nature masks an ability to make the best of any situation, no matter how challenging or unpleasant it may be. Although you are frequently centered on your own concerns (the way most Arians are), you rarely ignore an opportunity to help or inspire others. You have a magnetic charisma. You don't mind the ups and downs of life because you prefer to be caught up in extremes rather than dull routine.

**Embrace:** Reality; temperance; generous impulses

**Avoid:** Insincerity; impractical hope; valuing only what you can see

**Also born on this day:** Political commentator Rachel Maddow; actors Ali MacGraw and Debbie Reynolds; composer Sergei Rachmaninoff; writer Edgar Wallace

# April 2 • Aries

You walk a fine line between what you know of life and what you wish to be true. You possess uncanny powers of imagination and may spend a great deal of your life dreaming with eyes wide open. Your natural dignity may cause you to seem stand-offish to those who don't know you well. This reticence has a lordly resonance and creates an aura of specialness around you. You have confidence in your own ability to succeed and are slow to believe that anything happens by chance. A series of carefully planned moves and strategies helps you achieve your life plans, and you will adhere stringently to those plans at any cost.

**Embrace:** Wholesome values; a spiritual path; getting the most out of life

**Avoid:** Predictability; jealousy; boredom

**Also born on this day:** Writer Hans Christian Andersen; auto pioneer Walter Chrysler; singer Marvin Gaye; actor Alec Guinness

# April 3 • Aries

You have a broad view of life and see yourself as a citizen of the world. Although you may like to think of yourself as a social rebel, the truth is something quite different. You always manage in some way to draw upon the resources of the status quo to fund or support your iconoclastic aims. Individuals born on April 3 love taking chances in all avenues of life, and this includes the professional arena. High-stakes choices offer the thrills you seek. You have great ambition, and almost a sixth sense about making the right choice at the right time.

**Embrace:** Empathy; happy talk; spiritual values

**Avoid:** Coldheartedness; envy; empty praise

**Also born on this day:** Actors Alec Baldwin, Eddie Murphy, and Marlon Brando; singer/actor Doris Day; naturalist Jane Goodall; businesswoman Mellody Hobson; German chancellor Helmut Kohl

# April 4 • Aries

You are marked by a quiet strength, and you possess the enviable talent of being able to be worldly and spiritual in equal measure. You inspire through example, yet you never seek to force others into your way of thinking or behaving. A particular talent or ability is the keystone of your nature, yet you prefer to see yourself as many-faceted rather than singularly directed. You respond well under pressure and make your greatest strides when the deck is stacked against you.

**Embrace:** Self-worth; feeling good; the high road

**Avoid:** Trespassing on someone's feelings; arbitration; empty calories

**Also born on this day:** Poet Maya Angelou; composer Elmer Bernstein; actors Robert Downey Jr., Heath Ledger, and Anthony Perkins; Blues musician Muddy Waters

# April 5 • Aries

Those born on April 5 are the natural aristocrats among people. You have a high opinion of yourself and may even be self-centered, although that attitude in no way influences your ability to interact with others or to be likable. You have a lively intelligence and curiosity. Your best trait is unabashed honesty. You believe that there is nothing you can't achieve if you work hard and plan well. You don't look for success and good fortune to fall from the sky; instead, you're willing to sacrifice to make your dreams come true.

**Embrace:** Vitality; well-wishers; your soulmate

**Avoid:** Self-pity; capriciousness; overthinking

**Also born on this day:** Actors Bette Davis, Gregory Peck, and Spencer Tracy; U.S. Secretary of State Colin Powell; education pioneer Booker T. Washington; singer/songwriter/producer Pharrell Williams

# April 6 • Aries

Creativity and imagination of the highest level characterize those born on April 6. You are enormously talented and will use that talent as a means of expressing your life energy. You have the ability to convince others of your opinions and aims, yet the manner in which you accomplish this is subtle and generally displayed rather than uttered. You have faith that the good you do will be returned to you, and for this reason you make it your business to promote a positive attitude in all areas of life.

**Embrace:** Good luck; spiritual transcendence; integrity

**Avoid:** Constant worry; superficial relationships; gossip

**Also born on this day:** Composer/conductor André Previn; actors Zach Braff, Paul Rudd, and Billy Dee Williams

# April 7 • Aries

You are a fascinating combination of dreamer and doer, and you will always put your talents to work in improving the conditions of those around you. You have the ability to sense other people's feelings and can become involved in others' problems and concerns while withholding judgment. Your dreams and goals, like most facets of your life, are played out on a huge scale with drama to spare. Although practicality is not usually one of your strengths, you can put this skill to work if your desire to succeed is great enough.

**Embrace:** A new you; seeing the glass half full; artistic integrity

**Avoid:** Empty promises; selling yourself short; fatalism

**Also born on this day:** Actors Jackie Chan and Russell Crowe; film director Francis Ford Coppola; singer Billie Holiday; poet William Wordsworth

# April 8 • Aries

Despite a pleasing personality, you have steel at your core and never miss a chance to learn from your mistakes. You may be regarded as a potential mover and shaker, though your interests are often on a more limited scale. You don't see yourself as a catalyst for change but will endeavor to right a wrong if an opportunity presents itself. Your moral and spiritual sturdiness is a positive factor as you strive to achieve your dreams. No one can convince you that a goal is unreachable—even if you face enormous challenges, you do not give up and you do not complain.

**Embrace:** Bonding with loved ones; trust; entertainment

**Avoid:** Promiscuity; insensitivity; burning bridges

**Also born on this day:** Diplomat Kofi Annan; First Lady Betty Ford; actors Patricia Arquette, Mary Pickford, and Robin Wright

# April 9 • Aries

Feisty and opinionated, you see life as a series of missions, some of which are successful, some of which fail. More pragmatic than idealistic, you enjoy striving almost as much as you enjoy the victories your efforts bring. Your intrepid nature makes you a virtual pioneer who is not afraid to challenge the status quo. You know what you want out of life and aren't afraid to go after it. You are intensely loyal and will always stand by a friend, especially one who is in trouble. You accentuate the positive and don't often consider that a much-prized goal may not materialize.

**Embrace:** Going the distance; peace and joy; good taste

**Avoid:** Looking back; saying, "I told you so"; blaming others

**Also born on this day:** Poet Charles Baudelaire; singer/songwriter Carl Perkins; actors Jean-Paul Belmondo, Cynthia Nixon, Kristen Stewart, and Dennis Quaid

# April 10 • Aries

You're a fighter, though your sunny personality may obscure this fact. You have your own way of doing things, and you're unlikely to change your attitude in order to accommodate others. Though you manage to accomplish your aims in the nicest possible way, there is never any doubt about how ambitious you are. You have the capacity to see the world around you realistically, without letting that knowledge disillusion you. You truly adore people and consider your experiences with loved ones to be among the cherished moments of your life. When good things happen to you, you feel obligated to bestow good fortune on someone else.

**Embrace:** Simplicity; living in the now; friendliness

**Avoid:** Manipulative people; indiscretions; giving in too easily

**Also born on this day:** Ambassador/writer Clare Boothe Luce; coach/sportscaster John Madden; publisher Joseph Pulitzer; actors Harry Morgan, Haley Joel Osment, Steven Seagal, and Omar Sharif

# April 11 • Aries

Good-hearted and daring, people born on this date have the potential to do a great deal of good in the world. Whether you seek the broad arena of political activism or confine your involvement to your proverbial "own backyard," you display the care and compassion that is too often missing from human endeavors. You like to surround yourself with equals—partners who share your sense of commitment to your own goals and causes. You believe in your own ability to change the world. Even if specific goals go unfulfilled, you know how to turn a negative experience into a lesson learned.

**Embrace:** The rights of others; the pleasure of giving; enthusiasm

**Avoid:** Seeking approval; focusing on weakness; controversy

**Also born on this day:** Designer Oleg Cassini; actor Joel Grey; singer Lisa Stansfield; musician Joss Stone; poet Mark Strand

# April 12 • Aries

Armed with considerable intelligence, curiosity, and drive, you are in a class by yourself. You are a philosophical type who prizes learning, yet you don't confuse it with wisdom. You are a student of the human condition and a keen observer who can easily spot deception. You have a genuine gift for enjoying life, and your ability to laugh at yourself is refreshing. When you set your sights on a goal and make a commitment to it, you possess the will and ambition to make it a reality.

**Embrace:** The joy of giving; graceful words; daily affirmations

**Avoid:** Buying on credit; placing blame; seeing life from a single point of view

**Also born on this day:** Writers Tom Clancy and Beverly Cleary; musician Herbie Hancock; comedian/TV host David Letterman; actors Claire Danes, Shannen Doherty, Ed O'Neill, and Saoirse Ronan

# April 13 • Aries

There is definitely a spark of genius in people born on April 13. These are not showy individuals, but people who prefer existence in a humble—even obscure—setting. Although you would never seek fame, it sometimes finds you. When it does, it acts as a profound disruption in your life. You consider yourself at the service of others, but your analytic characteristics can make you seem rather cold. You go after what you want. Success and achievement may be rather abstract terms to you, but you realize that life is a game with many rules.

**Embrace:** An interest in others; seeing life through rose-colored glasses; long-range goals

**Avoid:** Family disputes; being a people-pleaser; arrogance

**Also born on this day:** U.S. president Thomas Jefferson; playwright Samuel Beckett; singer Al Green; journalist Christopher Hitchens; actors Paul Sorvino and Allison Williams

# April 14 • Aries

Your great desire is to be happy and at peace. You are highly evolved, emphatically intelligent, and rarely afraid to question, to search, to dream. You are capable of doing great things, yet the importance to you isn't in the act, but in how you can translate the experience into an illuminating life lesson.

**Embrace:** A rage to live; being yourself; laughter

**Avoid:** Taking things too seriously; antagonism; brooding over disappointments

**Also born on this day:** Actors Adrien Brody and Julie Christie; singer Loretta Lynn; baseball stars Greg Maddux and Pete Rose

# April 15 • Aries

Gifted and intuitive, you gain inspiration from the natural world. Even though you tend to accumulate material possessions, you are far more in tune with the meaningful aspects of life. You aspire to be loved above all else. You rely upon the acceptance of those who are dear to you.

**Embrace:** Cheerfulness; forgiveness; your own limitations

**Avoid:** Bragging; self-absorption; indecision

**Also born on this day:** Artist Leonardo da Vinci; novelist Henry James; Soviet leader Nikita Khrushchev; actor/writer Seth Rogen; actors Elizabeth Montgomery, Emma Thompson, and Emma Watson

# April 16 • Aries

You yearn to shine in the spotlight, even if only on a very small scale. You have an agenda and aren't afraid to advertise it. You want to reach the top and will work very hard to do so. This applies to your spiritual journey as well as lesser, material goals.

**Embrace:** Fantasies; musicality; taking chances

**Avoid:** Needing to win; delegating authority; jumping to conclusions

**Also born on this day:** Filmmaker/comedian Charlie Chaplin; actor Claire Foy; basketball star Kareem Abdul-Jabbar; composer Henry Mancini; singers Dusty Springfield and Bobby Vinton; aviator Wilbur Wright

# April 17 • Aries

You seem to have an innate understanding of the world around you and all of its intricacies, and you are always ready to seize an opportunity. When you state an opinion, everyone in your circle is certain to view it as wisdom. From an early age you display a marked ability for leadership and tend to select like-minded friends. Your goals and expectations are in line with your abilities. You are a hard worker, dedicated to carrying out your responsibilities as best you can. Failure and setbacks only make you more determined to succeed.

**Embrace:** Confidence; happy thoughts; emotional stability

**Avoid:** Guilt; self-criticism; danger

**Also born on this day:** Actors Sean Bean, Jennifer Garner, and William Holden; film director Adam McKay; financier J. P. Morgan; playwright Thornton Wilder

# April 18 • Aries

You are an eminent doer and achiever. When you set yourself a task, you will go to all lengths to accomplish it. Opinionated and aggressive, you often find yourself at the center of controversy. As long as there are causes to espouse and victories to be won, you are not the type to sit idly by. Your enthusiasm draws others to you. Your goal is to open the eyes of those around you and create change. An unswerving belief in your ability keeps you on track.

**Embrace:** Fun; personal accountability; positive ambiance

**Avoid:** Anger; hiding from the truth; attacking the motives of others

**Also born on this day:** Attorney Clarence Darrow; comedian/TV host Conan O'Brien; composer Miklós Rózsa; artist Max Weber; actors Barbara Hale, David Tennant, and James Woods

# April 19 • Aries

You possess a deep sense of your own spiritual significance and have the ability to do great things. You are not interested in making a public show of your very personal aims, yet the zeal that characterizes your ambition often gains you notice. Although you are not a great planner, you do have a natural instinct about what choices to make and when to make them. The decisions you make may seem curious to others, but you rarely question your intuition. You have a way of channeling your experiences and relationships into spiritual and intellectual growth.

**Embrace:** Second chances; a love of literature; gentleness

**Avoid:** Putting things off; disorganization; accepting failure too easily

**Also born on this day:** Actors Kate Hudson, Ashely Judd, and Jayne Mansfield; FBI crime-fighter Eliot Ness; designer Paloma Picasso; auto racer Al Unser Jr.

# April 20 • Aries

You are guided by your emotions. Even when you appear to make decisions based on logic and intellect, you are actually tapping into the rich pipeline of your subconscious mind. Because of your rich inner life, you sometimes appear to live in a dream world. Although naturally contemplative, you can summon the social élan needed to shine when the occasion arises. You tend to project your own needs and perceptions onto loved ones' personalities. Family is a strong force in your life. Involvement in socially significant projects gives you a sense of helping make the world a better place.

**Embrace:** Daydreams; making intelligent mistakes; true love

**Avoid:** Being overly serious; distractions; making enemies

**Also born on this day:** Actors Jessica Lange, Ryan O'Neal, and George Takei; baseball player/manager Don Mattingly; artist Joan Miró; Supreme Court Justice John Paul Stevens; singer Luther Vandross

# TAURUS

## April 21–May 20

Taurus is the second sign of the astrological year and is known by its symbol, the Bull. Taureans are loyal, thrifty, and kindhearted. With Venus as its ruling planet, people born under this sign typically possess great personal charm, good looks, and a lovely speaking voice. Luxury-loving and acquisitive, they also can be lazy.

Element: Earth
Planetary ruler: Venus
Key characteristic: Determination
Strengths: Hard working; honest; brave
Challenges: Intractable; short-sighted; bullying

# April 21 • Taurus

Your dynamism and sociability make you special. You have an interesting, spirited personality that attracts admirers in both your personal and professional life. You are extremely opinionated and at times have a problem accepting other points of view. Although your buoyant nature generally keeps you from seeming dogmatic or pushy, it's important that you cultivate tolerance on as broad a scale as you can muster. You're incredibly sentimental and romantic and believe that love was meant to last a lifetime. You believe in careful planning and are painstaking in your methods of bringing goals to fruition. You rarely let an opportunity go unfulfilled.

**Embrace:** The best of everything; growing old gracefully; letting go

**Avoid:** Fearing change; ignoring lessons; going for broke

**Also born on this day:** Novelist Charlotte Brontë; Russian empress Catherine the Great; naturalist John Muir; rocker Iggy Pop; Great Britain's Queen Elizabeth II

# April 22 • Taurus

There is a certain level of instability inherent in your character and personality, which makes you appealing and attractive in an offbeat way. Unusual circumstances and coincidences are the spice of life for you, and you may unconsciously draw excitement and danger into your life. Quirky and unconventional, you take life as it comes. The idea of plotting a course for success seems alien, even foolish, to you. You trust in your own ability to make choices that will bring you the satisfaction and fulfillment you want, as well as provide the excitement you need.

**Embrace:** Starting over; a good attitude; attention to detail

**Avoid:** Fear; interrupting; careless mistakes

**Also born on this day:** Philosopher Immanuel Kant; Soviet leader/Marxist revolutionary Vladimir Lenin; actor Jack Nicholson; physicist/father of the atomic bomb Robert Oppenheimer; pinup Bettie Page; filmmaker John Waters

# April 23 • Taurus

You have a brilliant and original mind. Your opinions generally run counter to conventional wisdom, and you don't care who disagrees with you. You are a joyous, irrepressible individual with the gift of making other people happy. You have so many interests that you give the impression of scattering your energies rather than channeling them. While this can be true occasionally, it suits your purpose, since variety, not constancy, is what makes your life worth living. You also take an active interest in helping people close to you realize their own dreams and goals.

**Embrace:** Industry; willingness to work; contentment

**Avoid:** Dishonest reasoning; irreverence; selfishness

**Also born on this day:** U.S. president James Buchanan; comedian/TV host John Oliver; singer Roy Orbison; playwright William Shakespeare; actor Shirley Temple; painter J. M. W. Turner

# April 24 • Taurus

People born on April 24 have a flair for the good life and a love of glamour. You are a practical individual who plays by the rules. You are also talented, with a good sense of humor and the ability to laugh at yourself. You have big dreams and the determination to mold those dreams into reality. People born on this date tend to formulate definite career plans at an early age. At the same time, you're practical and patient and don't mind making the sacrifices that come with high aspirations.

**Embrace:** Holistic healing; stylish apparel; competition

**Avoid:** Getting even; feeling unappreciated; making excuses

**Also born on this day:** Musician Doug Clifford; actor Shirley MacLaine; singer/actor Barbra Streisand; novelist Anthony Trollope

# April 25 • Taurus

You seek life's deepest mysteries, and this gives you a tolerance that few others possess. At your core is a great spirituality, which gives you amazing strength of character. When disappointment comes your way, you don't lose your natural composure; instead, you see the challenges as a valuable learning experience. Success to you has very little to do with accumulating worldly possessions or praise. It is the intangibles of life that concerns you, since you have no need of external validation. People born on April 25 can make extraordinary spiritual guides and mentors.

**Embrace:** Concentration; pondering an answer; playing for keeps

**Avoid:** Tension; telling a hurtful truth; worrying about death

**Also born on this day:** Singer Ella Fitzgerald; basketball star Meadowlark Lemon; journalist Edward R. Murrow; actors Hank Azaria, Al Pacino, and Renée Zellweger

# April 26 • Taurus

There is a serious side to you that isn't always noticeable beneath your amiable exterior. You have fine judgment and possess an instinct for making just the right decision at the opportune time. You take your relationships very seriously and your ability to inspire sincere affection helps to explain why your friends are so devoted to you. You believe in old-fashioned values. To you, success is always the result of hard work. You have a healthy respect for talent and ability, and you don't think that anything meaningful can be accomplished without sacrifice.

**Embrace:** Leisure; giving yourself the benefit of the doubt; spiritual thinking

**Avoid:** Self-interest; emotional detachment; snobbishness

**Also born on this day:** Artist/ornithologist John James Audubon; actor/comedian Carol Burnett; landscape architect Frederick Law Olmsted; architect I. M. Pei

# April 27 • Taurus

You are a study in extremes. Your emotions run hot and cold, and you have a reputation for being temperamental when crossed. Though you are intelligent, you are primarily a doer, not a thinker. Instinct plays a big part in guiding your decision-making, and you are famous for saying what you think. You are people-oriented and never seem to run out of enthusiasm. You are a natural cheerleader for worthy causes. Your personality is forceful, sometimes overwhelming, yet your heart is always in the right place. You believe fervently in your dreams and your ability to realize them.

**Embrace:** High energy; faithfulness; charity work

**Avoid:** Boastfulness; being argumentative; making enemies

**Also born on this day:** U.S. president Ulysses S. Grant; baseball player/manager Rogers Hornsby; radio personality Casey Kasem; civil rights activist Coretta Scott King; inventor Samuel Morse; playwright August Wilson

# April 28 • Taurus

You have an amazing capacity for living life to the fullest and never fail to recognize an opportunity that comes your way. People born on this day are firm believers in the "glass is half full" philosophy. There is no cynicism in your nature, and you can find logic and reason in even the most difficult, trying circumstances. You derive a great deal of happiness from your friends' joys and successes. You tend to identify strongly with your career identity, especially if there are other areas of your life that are not yielding all the promise you expected.

**Embrace:** Taking care of yourself; a good attitude; time

**Avoid:** Self-pity; laziness; disenchantment

**Also born on this day:** Entertainer Ann-Margret; actors Jessica Alba, Lionel Barrymore, and Penélope Cruz; novelist Harper Lee; comedian/TV host Jay Leno; U.S. president James Monroe; industrialist Oskar Schindler

# April 29 • Taurus

You are concerned with how others perceive you. This isn't the result of an unhealthy ego; rather, you simply have a high level of sensitivity, and literally "feel" the approval or disapproval of those around you. Part of the problem is your inability to appreciate your own best character traits: Learning to believe in your own talents can be a tall order for you. You don't believe in superficial attachments. You're very loyal to your friends and are willing to go to extremes to offer help and support. You may be more ambitious than you are comfortable acknowledging.

**Embrace:** Liberality; ethics; being spontaneous

**Avoid:** Irrationality; loose talk; childish behavior

**Also born on this day:** Tennis champion Andre Agassi; auto racer Dale Earnhardt; musician Duke Ellington; publisher William Randolph Hearst; actors Daniel Day-Lewis, Michelle Pfeiffer, and Uma Thurman; comedian Jerry Seinfeld

# April 30 • Taurus

From an early age, your life-path has been influenced by outside forces. You enjoy living on a big—even massive—scale, with hopes and dreams to match. You tend to enjoy playing for high stakes in all aspects of life. You are ambitious and are continually working to make a success of your life, both personally and professionally. Unlike many others, you aren't fond of making heavy sacrifices in order to make your dreams come true. You believe you can have it all and generally end up having exactly that!

**Embrace:** Exploration; family values; living in the present

**Avoid:** Wasting resources; losing interest; self-indulgence

**Also born on this day:** Actors Eve Arden, Ana de Armas, Kirsten Dunst, and Cloris Leachman; composer Franz Lehár; basketball player Isiah Thomas; singer Bobby Vee

# May 1 • Taurus

You have an indomitable will and endless ambition. Your ambition has little ego attached to it, however, and is primarily a vehicle for the expression of personality. Your energy inspires everyone around you. Because of this you are a natural leader. You generally don't like being the center of attention. You're much more comfortable delegating authority than taking it for yourself. You bring out the best in your compatriots and are often responsible for helping your friends to make important, even vital decisions.

**Embrace:** Prayer; discipline; belief in others

**Avoid:** Lack of communication; competition; loneliness

**Also born on this day:** Filmmaker Wes Anderson; actor Glenn Ford; novelist Joseph Heller; Kamehameha I, king of Hawaii; musician/actor Tim McGraw; comedian/TV host Jack Paar

# May 2 • Taurus

You are fully aware of your unique gifts and want to share them with the world. Creativity—both artistic and intellectual—is your personal hallmark. Although you may seem cautious, you are an adventurous soul. You are brave about the choices you make in life. Helping the intangible become tangible is your major goal. You exist on the strength of your inner vision. In order to believe totally in that vision, you must see it manifested through an act of belief, a commitment to creativity.

**Embrace:** Partnership; appreciation of beauty; farewells

**Avoid:** Being docile; deception; incompatibility

**Also born on this day:** Actor Christine Baranski; soccer player David Beckham; singer Jon Bon Jovi; satirist Jerome K. Jerome; actor/wrestler Dwayne Johnson; pediatrician Dr. Benjamin Spock

# May 3 • Taurus

Power, and the means by which it is used and exchanged, are central factors in defining your life. You continually find yourself drawn to the very seat of power, though you may not desire to occupy it yourself. You want very much to help others through your own experiences, but first you must come to grips with some of the truths in your life. You are determined to make good use of all the opportunities that come your way. Not particularly intuitive, you depend upon logic to point the way.

**Embrace:** Delight; a sense of community; bliss

**Avoid:** Material gratification; emotional isolation; chaos

**Also born on this day:** Actor Mary Astor; singers James Brown, Bing Crosby, and Pete Seeger; political philosopher/writer Niccolò Machiavelli; boxer Sugar Ray Robinson

# May 4 • Taurus

Where most people tend to complicate events, you want to enjoy life in a simple, unadorned fashion. Although it may take many years for you to throw off the burdens that keep you from exploring life on your own terms, you will eventually come to this point of view. Your charismatic personality sets you apart. You are a philosophical type who asks "Why not?" when contemplating a life change. You tend to work harder in aid of others than for yourself. You don't flaunt your possessions or make a great display of your charitable works. You often choose to do good work in silence.

**Embrace:** Interesting projects; joy; changes of venue

**Avoid:** Anxiety; insecurity; drawing conclusions

**Also born on this day:** Sportscaster Erin Andrews; actors Will Arnett and Audrey Hepburn; golfer Rory McIlroy; singer Randy Travis

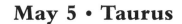

# May 5 • Taurus

Individuals born on this day have a definite agenda in mind. You are verbal, imaginative, and not at all shy about expressing your opinions. You are also a good listener, and despite your "chatty" reputation, you can keep a secret better than most people. You identify more with your intellect than with any other aspect of your nature. You never stop learning and never want to close the book on achieving the very best you can. You are adventurous, and you are looking to establish a "personal best" that accords with your own standards—not those of anyone else.

**Embrace:** Self-motivation; gladness; justice

**Avoid:** Living in a dream world; glib remarks; apathy

**Also born on this day:** Singer/songwriter Adele; investigative journalist Nellie Bly; political philosopher Karl Marx; comedian/actor Michael Palin; singer Tammy Wynette

# May 6 • Taurus

Where life goals are concerned, many people born on this date are late starters. You may be able to coast through the first half of your life on charm, and you often don't begin to show your grit until after you've weathered a few disappointments. What you really want most is to be taken seriously. You are more likely to be a trailblazer than a traditionalist. You have an intense side, but it is rarely visible except to those who know you best. You have real star quality, and you know how to use it to get what you want out of life.

**Embrace:** Smiles; surprises; happily ever after

**Avoid:** Pretense; empty promises; casual sex

**Also born on this day:** British prime minister Tony Blair; psychoanalysis founder Sigmund Freud; actors George Clooney and Rudolph Valentino; baseball star Willie Mays; director/actor Orson Welles

# May 7 • Taurus

You know how to love, serve, and wait. You are highly principled, and your concern for others typically outweighs concern for yourself. Your ability to put your own quiet strength behind the people you love is remarkable. Those born on May 7 are the most loved and loving people in the world. You tend to keep your hopes and dreams to yourself. Generally, you wish to make a success of your important relationships and maintain the clarity of your creative inspiration. No amount of money can substitute for the satisfaction you require in your life's work.

**Embrace:** Diversity; entertainment; transition periods

**Avoid:** Idle talk; envying others; ill-mannered behavior

**Also born on this day:** Poet Robert Browning; actor Gary Cooper; Argentine first lady Eva Perón; TV journalist/host Tim Russert; composer Pyotr Ilich Tchaikovsky; football quarterback Johnny Unitas

# May 8 • Taurus

You are practical and intelligent in a commonsense way. While rarely glamorous, you have the opportunity to make a name for yourself by the very nature of your capableness. You are well-known for your sense of humor. You can recognize the funny side of any situation, and you have a reputation for saying what you think, whether it's critical or complimentary. You don't believe in waiting for goals to come true—you go out and grab them. An exceptionally organized person, you are likely to plan your goals carefully, and never expect anything to be given to you without some intense effort and a few sacrifices on your part.

**Embrace:** Soulfulness; intelligence; love of nature

**Avoid:** Pressure; nervousness; loneliness

**Also born on this day:** Naturalist David Attenborough; novelist Peter Benchley; singer/songwriter Enrique Iglesias; U.S. president Harry S. Truman; poet Phillis Wheatley

# May 9 • Taurus

People born on May 9 are warriors in every sense of the word. You possess a bold spirit that propels you toward challenges that other, more timid individuals would never face. Despite the forcefulness of your personality, you are by no means pushy or even aggressive. Your enthusiasm level is extremely high, and you have the ability to laugh at yourself. There is no hidden agenda with you—what you see is what you get. You have a talent for leadership and great entrepreneurial skills, and may seek to start your own business.

**Embrace:** Gentility; a sense of humor; color

**Avoid:** Preoccupation with death; boredom; pretentiousness

**Also born on this day:** Playwright James Barrie; film director James L. Brooks; abolitionist John Brown; actors Candice Bergen, Rosario Dawson, and Glenda Jackson; singer Billy Joel; newscaster Mike Wallace

# May 10 • Taurus

You have a special view of the world. You are a cautious optimist and believe that if you try hard enough, you can make a positive impact upon your world. Though you aren't naturally a solitary person, you do require more than your share of privacy. You live out your dreams and goals on an everyday basis, relying on your subconscious to give you the guidance you need. You have very high expectations about your ability to turn failure into success, and you may sometimes subconsciously hinder your own efforts in order to test your ability to "come back."

**Embrace:** Critical thinking; preparedness; mental toughness

**Avoid:** Risky behavior; naïveté; shame

**Also born on this day:** Dancer/actor Fred Astaire; musicians Bono, Donovan, and Sid Vicious; fashion designer Miuccia Prada; film-score composer Max Steiner

# May 11 • Taurus

Few people have the overwhelming creative potential that you possess. Whether or not you turn your talents toward artistic expression, you will be known for your ability to turn the ordinary into the special. You are brilliant, talented—and somewhat volatile. Despite a reputation for being short-tempered, even critical, you command the loyalty and devotion of everyone who knows you. There is no limit to how big you can dream. You believe in your talent, and although sometimes assailed by doubts of how strictly you can adhere to the practical demands involved in bringing goals to fruition, you have far more grit than is generally supposed.

**Embrace:** Permanence; hidden talents; graciousness

**Avoid:** Negative influences; grudges; favoritism

**Also born on this day:** Songwriter Irving Berlin; artist Salvador Dalí; pilot Harriet Quimby; actor Natasha Richardson

# May 12 • Taurus

You are not so much a leader as you are a guide, eager to show others the world through your eyes. You appreciate the serious aspects of life, even though you seem to be caught up in the pure pleasure of living it. You have boundless energy and give equal amounts to both work and play. You believe in setting reachable goals. Your enjoyment and enthusiasm show in everything you do. Although you don't need to be the center of attention, you generally are. Many of your associates try to emulate your charm and good-natured appeal.

**Embrace:** Clean living; memory; your own style

**Avoid:** Repetition; sarcasm; becoming notorious

**Also born on this day:** Composer Burt Bacharach; baseball legend Yogi Berra; comedian George Carlin; actors Emilio Estevez, Katharine Hepburn, and Rami Malek; skateboarder Tony Hawk; poet Edward Lear; nurse Florence Nightingale

# May 13 • Taurus

You are a rare individual with unique and special talents. You have great imaginative potential, which you may need to shape through learning and experience. You have a naturally giving nature and the ability to put your trust in someone close to you. You are quick to reveal your thoughts and feelings, and you enjoy talking about shared goals. To be better able to accomplish your goals, keep a specific direction in mind. There is a dark side to you, yet you are rarely moved to show this aspect of yourself to anyone.

**Embrace:** Reliability; pride; kindness to animals

**Avoid:** Senseless arguments; overspending; tension

**Also born on this day:** Comedian/TV host Stephen Colbert; actor/writer/producer Lena Dunham; boxer Joe Louis; novelist Daphne du Maurier; basketball player Dennis Rodman; musician Stevie Wonder

# May 14 • Taurus

You are torn between the intellectual life to which you are drawn and the active life you want to pursue. This dichotomy of choice and personality is the defining factor in your life. You have extraordinary artistic vision and can do great things if left to your own devices. You have a very specific idea of what constitutes success. On the one hand you value your own assessment of personal achievement, yet you also value the approval of others, particularly respected colleagues. You are self-critical and must learn that external validation is not the true measure of your success.

**Embrace:** The ability to apologize; happy thoughts; starting over

**Avoid:** Rage; confusion; lack of imagination

**Also born on this day:** Actor Cate Blanchett; singer Bobby Darin; filmmaker George Lucas; Facebook founder Mark Zuckerberg

# May 15 • Taurus

You draw inspiration from your physical and emotional surroundings. You have a great need to distill your experience and share it with others through art or some other personal expression. You are a natural do-gooder who likes to feel thoroughly connected to the world family. Success has many faces and you are not always sure just which of these appeal to you. You have many dreams, but it can be difficult for you to focus on a definite plan to make your dreams reality.

**Embrace:** Transcendental awareness; mental energy; ecstasy

**Avoid:** Bitterness; emotional stability; lies

**Also born on this day:** U.S. Secretary of State Madeleine Albright; novelist L. Frank Baum; baseball star George Brett; musician Brian Eno; artist Jasper Johns; football players Ray Lewis and Emmitt Smith; playwright Peter Shaffer

# May 16 • Taurus

People born on May 16 are among the most buoyant and fascinating personalities within the entire spectrum of astrology. You have your own view of life and your own style—both of which set you apart. You can seem argumentative because you enjoy exchanging opinions with others. You prefer a rousing argument to a quiet discussion. You are an innovator and value your freedom of choice above everything else. You see no point in maintaining tradition just for its own sake.

**Embrace:** A sense of history; good sportsmanship; belief

**Avoid:** Picking fights with friends; attitude problems; shallowness

**Also born on this day:** Actors Pierce Brosnan and Henry Fonda; gymnast Olga Korbut; pianist Liberace; fashion designer Christian Lacroix; baseball player/manager Billy Martin; author Studs Terkel

# May 17 • Taurus

You enjoy the pursuit of excellence. You are a self-starter, and you know what you want and how to get it. You will not allow yourself to be diverted from achieving your goals. You are intelligent, though not showy about what you know; for this reason, you may not be perceived as especially brilliant by others. That's fine with you, since you are considerably less concerned with how your actions are perceived by others than with whether you yourself are content. Because you have considerable leadership potential, you are likely to surround yourself with more "followers" than equals.

**Embrace:** Staying power; morality; daydreams

**Avoid:** Inconsistency; guilt; truculence

**Also born on this day:** Watergate prosecutor Archibald Cox; actors Dennis Hopper, Maureen O'Sullivan, and Bill Paxton; boxer Sugar Ray Leonard; comedian/actor Bob Saget

# May 18 • Taurus

Love of freedom and independence characterizes people born on May 18. You are temperamental, lovable, and exasperating; you make it impossible for others to be indifferent toward you. You possess extraordinary creative energy and are never without an important cause to champion. You enjoy taking risks, but only when you believe the risk "matters." You are deceptively ambitious—a fact that may go unnoticed by everyone except those who know you best. You are extremely emotional and no stranger to heartache. You are wise and understand that heartache often brings a measure of wisdom.

**Embrace:** Dreams; good taste; criticism

**Avoid:** Rationalization; anxiety; feeling guilty

**Also born on this day:** Film director Frank Capra; actor/comedian Tina Fey; Pope John Paul II; baseball players Reggie Jackson and Brooks Robinson

# May 19 • Taurus

You came into this world wanting to change it. You are extremely motivated, eager to put your personal stamp upon your environment. You have supreme confidence in your abilities and never shrink when it comes to doing what is expected of you. You are a loner, but not in the traditional sense. You enjoy being with people, yet you trust only your own counsel and rarely take the advice of others. Resourceful? You're at the head of the line. That old adage "there are no small parts, only small actors" could have been written to describe you.

**Embrace:** Jokes; simplicity; true love

**Avoid:** Nightmares; taking foolish chances; losing faith

**Also born on this day:** Screenwriter/film director Nora Ephron; basketball players Kevin Garnett and Dolph Schayes; musician Pete Townshend; activist Malcolm X

# May 20 • Taurus

You have a streak of eccentricity in your otherwise conventional personality. You seem to draw friends from all walks of life. You love to listen to anyone's story and are famous for giving remarkably apt advice. You have a need to display your talents on a very large scale, yet this may be in conflict with your basic need for emotional privacy. You are ambitious, yet you may lack the emotional stamina needed to be successful in your chosen field. You may have an unrealistic attitude about what it takes to make your dreams come true.

**Embrace:** Challenges; good causes; peace of mind

**Avoid:** Negative attitude; running away from problems; lack of respect for reasonable authority

**Also born on this day:** Singer/actor Cher; singer Joe Cocker; philosopher John Stuart Mill; actor Jimmy Stewart

# GEMINI

## May 21–June 20

◇०-◈-०·····························०-◈-०◇

Gemini is the third sign of the astrological year and is known by its astrological symbol, the Twins. Gemini individuals are bright, changeable, and inquiring. With Mercury as the ruling planet, people born under this sign are considered to quick thinkers who are always in motion. They have many interests and great social adeptness.

**Element:** Air
**Planetary ruler:** Mercury
**Key characteristic:** Communication
**Strengths:** Witty; talkative; versatile
**Challenges:** Superficial; fickle; unwilling to commit

# May 21 • Gemini

You have a great will to succeed, and you bend all your efforts toward that aim. Although you may not be especially good at articulating your goals, you have a very clear idea of what you want out of life. Security is usually very high on the list, and you will work hard to ensure it. You see things on a grand—even epic—scale and live your life in a similar fashion. Because of your dedication and sense of purpose, you may be perceived as ruthless at times. However, you are extremely generous and always willing to help out.

**Embrace:** Sophistication; physical exertion; progressive thinking

**Avoid:** Backtracking; irascibility; inflated speech

**Also born on this day:** Actors Raymond Burr and Mr. T; football player/ coach Ara Parseghian; poet Alexander Pope; painter Henri Rousseau; musician Fats Waller

# May 22 • Gemini

You have great charisma and the ability to draw attention to yourself. Also, you possess something of a dual nature: You may be lofty and intellectual one day, earthy and intense on another. You are generally seen as a leader, though you may not see yourself in this role. You are proud to see your hard work rewarded. You don't believe in getting something for nothing and would not wish to have idle dreams come true. But when you work very hard toward a goal—especially if it requires the discipline of many years—you are ecstatic.

**Embrace:** A healing spirit; perfection; balance

**Avoid:** Being quarrelsome; self-interest; obsession

**Also born on this day:** Painter Mary Cassatt; tennis player Novak Djokovic; writer Sir Arthur Conan Doyle; politician/activist Harvey Milk; actor Sir Laurence Olivier; oil tycoon T. Boone Pickens; composer Richard Wagner

# May 23 • Gemini

People born on May 23 are known for their sense of humor and sense of style. You are a fun-loving and free-thinking person who you enjoys life on your terms. Even more than most Geminians, you embody a youthful attitude. You are highly idealistic and spend a great deal of time daydreaming.

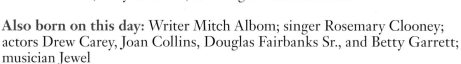

**Embrace:** The will to win; life-lessons; loss

**Avoid:** Artifice; risky behavior; dwelling on bad memories

**Also born on this day:** Writer Mitch Albom; singer Rosemary Clooney; actors Drew Carey, Joan Collins, Douglas Fairbanks Sr., and Betty Garrett; musician Jewel

# May 24 • Gemini

Despite the placid face you turn to the world, you have a strong intellect and rock-hard opinions. You are well suited to handling the stresses and strains of life, even though you may appear to be emotionally fragile. You nearly always manage to get your way, yet you do it with subtlety and diplomacy.

**Embrace:** Plentitude; joint ventures; negotiation

**Avoid:** Emotional temptation; ego trips; giving in to writer's block

**Also born on this day:** Singer Rosanne Cash; cinematographer Roger Deakins; singer/songwriter Bob Dylan; actor John C. Reilly; Queen Victoria of Great Britain

# May 25 • Gemini

You are energetic and focused, and you enjoy being in life's fast lane. You have enormous ambition to succeed and put career plans ahead of your personal relationships. You are creative in a quirky way, preferring to put your unique spin on events rather than allowing yourself to be ruled by any given circumstance.

**Embrace:** Symbolism; appreciation of nature; knowledge

**Avoid:** Jealousy; carelessness with money; putting off necessary chores

**Also born on this day:** Poet Ralph Waldo Emerson; novelist Robert Ludlum; actors Anne Heche and Sir Ian McKellen; comedian/actor Mike Myers

# May 26 • Gemini

Your natural character is hard for others to divine. Outwardly you appear serious—even stoic. Yet underneath it all, you are warm-hearted, kind, and even funny. You are highly aware of your own dignity. Even the way you carry yourself proclaims a sense of decorum. Friendship is one of the most important factors in your life. You have a knack for making close, lifelong friendships. You are extremely loyal and would do anything for a friend. You understand that very few goals can be achieved overnight. You have the foresight and patience to achieve your dreams one step at a time.

**Embrace:** Comfort; conversations with yourself; solitude

**Avoid:** Pragmatism; estrangement from friends; self-pity

**Also born on this day:** Actors Helena Bonham Carter and John Wayne; astronaut Sally Ride; musicians Miles Davis, Lenny Kravitz, Stevie Nicks, and Hank Williams Jr.

# May 27 • Gemini

You are a master at reinventing yourself. This is your way of remaining interesting to yourself and others. You never quite let anyone see your true self—not even those individuals closest to you. You love the spotlight and especially enjoy situations where you can meet new and interesting people. You like eccentric people who share your love of good food and smart conversation. You will usually find a way to shine, since anything less is unbearable to your ego. You are a natural flirt, and you generally prefer "the chase" to any other aspect of love.

**Embrace:** Emotional restoration; quiet joys; mystery

**Avoid:** Intimidation; snobbishness; misinformation

**Also born on this day:** Marine biologist/writer Rachel Carson; writer Dashiell Hammett; U.S. Secretary of State Henry Kissinger; actors Joseph Fiennes and Vincent Price; golfer Sam Snead; business magnate Cornelius Vanderbilt

# May 28 • Gemini

You possess an adventurous pioneer spirit. You don't wait for life to happen to you—you go out and wrestle with it. You never lose interest in life, and you are confident in your ability to conquer it. Enthusiastic and fun-loving, you are a great friend. You count your successes according to the number of lives you touch and people you inspire—and how much fun everybody has along the way. You believe in performing selfless acts of charity that improve the lives of others. This, combined with unstinting good humor, is your trademark.

**Embrace:** Safe arrivals; a happy heart; a winning spirit

**Avoid:** Bad dreams; revenge; nervousness

**Also born on this day:** Novelist Ian Fleming; politician Rudy Giuliani; singer Gladys Knight; Olympian Jim Thorpe; guitarist/singer/songwriter T-Bone Walker; basketball player Jerry West

# May 29 • Gemini

You possess charm, intelligence, wit, and a star quality that is virtually unrivaled. Your ability to sway the opinions of others is nothing short of miraculous. If you lack for anything, it is an introspective side. You prefer not to analyze your feelings except on rare occasions. You gravitate to risk and can even be foolhardy at times. You are extremely goal-oriented and will work very hard to make a goal become a reality. If you get bored along the way, however, you will toss all your hard work to the wind without a second thought.

**Embrace:** High style; wholeness; humility

**Avoid:** Self-parody; aloofness; overlooking areas that need your attention

**Also born on this day:** Actor Annette Bening; musicians Melissa Etheridge and Noel Gallagher; American patriot Patrick Henry; entertainer Bob Hope; U.S. president John F. Kennedy

# May 30 • Gemini

You are like an artist who sees the entire world as your canvas. You have considerable mettle and can overcome adversity with ease. You bring a great sense of joy and comfort to all of your relationships. Your will to succeed is strong but never ruthless. You have a knack for organization and use this talent in every aspect of life. You are scrupulously honest. You live by very high standards of personal conduct. You are proud of your ethics and may feel a need to convince others to follow a similar path.

**Embrace:** Good grooming; riches of the soul; attention to detail

**Avoid:** Indifference; sleeplessness; poor choices

**Also born on this day:** Musician Benny Goodman; film director Howard Hawks; singer Wynonna Judd; cosmonaut Alexey Leonov; football player Gale Sayers

# May 31 • Gemini

You like to push the proverbial envelope, always looking for ways to get close to dangerous circumstances without actually getting hurt. You like to give others the impression that you have a "bad" streak, but generally you're not as unconventional as you may appear. People born on May 31 like to live in the "now." You are not a deliberate planner. You take life as it comes and don't worry too much about the consequences. Success is an abstract concept to you, defined more by attitude than capitulation to a prescribed set of rules.

**Embrace:** Putting first things first; following your dream; being at ease

**Avoid:** The need for validation; no-win situations; giving up

**Also born on this day:** Actor/director Clint Eastwood; football quarterback Joe Namath; Prince Rainier of Monaco; model/actor Brooke Shields; poet Walt Whitman

# June 1 • Gemini

You need to bask in the sun of approval. You value your talents and abilities, yet you constantly look to your peers for validation and advice. Feeling that you have the power to please others is as seductive to you as your own success. People born on June 1 crave achievement and attention. You believe that success equals happiness and are often unhappy with life if you feel it doesn't measure up to your youthful goals. You possess incredible optimism and are likely to hold out for your dream job rather than take something you don't like.

**Embrace:** Lightening someone's burden; higher education; posterity

**Avoid:** Excessive interdependence; empty promises; scheming

**Also born on this day:** Singer Pat Boone; hockey player Paul Coffey; supermodel Heidi Klum; actors Morgan Freeman and Marilyn Monroe; singer/songwriter Alanis Morissette; comedian Amy Schumer

# June 2 • Gemini

You live more through your emotions than your intellect. This may not be readily apparent, since you are a bright achiever with a quiet personality that discourages you from "opening up"; you reserve your real self for those closest to you. You have a more serious disposition than many Geminians. You give the impression of being emotionally fragile, but you are actually very strong-willed and independent. You are not interested in superficial relationships of any sort; to the contrary, you seek out friends who can share your need for emotional intimacy.

**Embrace:** Acts of daring; professional advice; adaptability

**Avoid:** Doubts; constant criticism (of self and others); gloating

**Also born on this day:** Actor Wayne Brady; composer Edward Elgar; novelist Thomas Hardy; golfer Charlie Sifford; soccer player Abby Wambach; musician Charlie Watts; philosopher/activist Cornel West

# June 3 • Gemini

People born on June 3 are extremely intelligent, though their brilliance is likely to be analytical rather than creative in nature. You are much more at home analyzing abstract issues rather than handling life's more commonplace problems. You have considerable nervous energy, which can manifest itself as ill temper. Although you can be argumentative at times, you are much more likely to keep your feelings to yourself. There is an element of egotism in your persona, yet it does not detract from your likability. Friends admire your intellect. It's important to you that you achieve a level of independence in your personal and professional life.

**Embrace:** Intellect; making others happy; egoless love

**Avoid:** Selfishness; emotional power plays; needless fear

**Also born on this day:** Singer/dancer Josephine Baker; TV journalist Anderson Cooper; basketball player/coach Billy Cunningham; poet Allen Ginsberg; musician Curtis Mayfield; tennis champion Rafael Nadal

# June 4 • Gemini

You think of life as one big series of exciting surprises, and you are not afraid to take chances or reinvent yourself from time to time. You combine daring with practicality, discipline with artistry. This all comes naturally to you because of your incredible ability to see things from multiple perspectives. You have a sparkling personality and are very much aware of the effect you have on others. You love spontaneity and would rather be caught off guard by circumstances than plan for them. One of your greatest traits is your humanitarianism—you feel it is your duty to give your resources and talents to help those who are less fortunate.

**Embrace:** Charity; quietude; turning the other cheek

**Avoid:** Giving in to disillusionment; scheming; codependency

**Also born on this day:** Opera singer Cecilia Bartoli; comedian Russell Brand; Great Britain's King George III; actor Angelina Jolie

# June 5 • Gemini

You believe in the natural goodness of the world around you, and you have a remarkable ability to see things in a positive light. You want to experience everything life has to offer. You are more than merely optimistic—you are an altruist who draws inspiration from the magic of everyday life that others may not perceive. You like being surrounded by good companions and rarely prefer your own company. Your goals are optimistic in nature—sometimes impossibly so. But this does not deter you. If a dream doesn't come true, you simply turn your attention to the next goal.

**Embrace:** Fantasy; tears of joy; patience

**Avoid:** Wasting time; judging others; letting tasks overwhelm you

**Also born on this day:** Musician Kenny G; economist John Maynard Keynes; journalist Bill Moyers

# June 6 • Gemini

You are a remarkable individual for whom the world is one gigantic wonder to be explored. You have unbounded curiosity and never tire of learning new things. With so many artistic talents at your disposal, you can easily make a place for yourself in some creative field. People born on June 6 are dreamers. You often set goals for yourself that seem impossible, and yet on some level you are able to hit your mark. You understand what many people do not—that the journey is more important than the destination.

**Embrace:** Contentment; spiritual peace; tradition

**Avoid:** Tension; negativity; hopelessness

**Also born on this day:** Comedian Sandra Bernhard; tennis star Björn Borg; actor Paul Giamatti; American patriot Nathan Hale; novelist Thomas Mann

# June 7 • Gemini

You yearn to make your presence felt in the world, and you can get far in life just on your charm. You are curious and vibrant, with an ability to keep your level of enthusiasm high no matter what obstacles you encounter. You have a deservedly high opinion of yourself and will go to great lengths to make yourself seen and your views heard. You can put your creative abilities to good use in careers in the arts or humanities. People born on June 7 may opt for periods of worldly abstinence. You understand the importance of occasionally setting your sights on nonmaterialistic goals.

**Embrace:** Affection; spiritual escape; wondrous memories

**Avoid:** Greed; envy; dishonor

**Also born on this day:** Artist Paul Gauguin; basketball player Allen Iverson; singer Al Jolson; musician Prince; actors Liam Neeson and Jessica Tandy

# June 8 • Gemini

You are a survivor, with considerably more emotional stamina than the typical Gemini. No matter how many times you suffer setbacks or disappointments, you come back and start again. You are a hard worker who puts your whole heart and soul into everything you do. Your level of commitment is amazing. You have a gift for managing other people. You are adept at bringing out the best traits in others because you constantly emphasize the positive rather than the negative aspects of any given situation. Your goals may reflect a need to live up to the expectations of someone you admire.

**Embrace:** Confidence; wholesome enjoyment; conversation

**Avoid:** Pretense; laziness; giving in to discouragement

**Also born on this day:** Actor Julianna Margulies; comedian/TV host Joan Rivers; composer Robert Schumann; comedian Jerry Stiller; architect Frank Lloyd Wright

# June 9 • Gemini

You are motivated to succeed in every aspect of life. You are excitable and imaginative, with a great sense of humor. Like most Geminians, you are talkative and enjoy a rousing debate about a variety of subjects. You can have a good time in just about any situation; in fact, you are often the proverbial life of the party. You also have a serious side, but you usually keep it hidden. You use bold intelligence to put your plans into action from a very early age, and you have the daring to undertake risks that would intimidate other people.

**Embrace:** Innovations; courage; ethical behavior

**Avoid:** Self-pity; bossiness; manipulative people

**Also born on this day:** Actors Johnny Depp, Michael J. Fox, and Natalie Portman; comedian Jackie Mason; Russian tsar Peter the Great; composer/lyricist Cole Porter

# June 10 • Gemini

You have a highly emotional nature. You may seem to be on an endless roller coaster of highs and lows, which can both amaze and alarm those close to you. Although you seem very secure with your self-image, you are acutely aware of the expectations of others and may go to great lengths to live up to them. You have many goals and plans, yet you may not always feel confident you have what it takes to realize them. You find it difficult to be truly happy unless you feel fulfilled on an emotional level as well as a spiritual one.

**Embrace:** Joy of living; moderation; quiet times

**Avoid:** Excesses; unstable love affairs; depression

**Also born on this day:** Author Saul Bellow; actor/singer Judy Garland; figure skater Tara Lipinski; actor Hattie McDaniel; Prince Philip, Duke of Edinburgh; author/illustrator Maurice Sendak

# June 11 • Gemini

Although you are not particularly goal-oriented, you have a strong personal vision about what you want your life to be. You know what you want out of life, and you have the ability to move beyond the commonplace. Even though you need a great deal of personal validation from others, you possess an ego strong enough to support your grandiose ambitions. You have leadership qualities that are second to none. Properly focused, you have the potential to make a real difference in the world. You have a great deal of faith in your own abilities and will work very hard to make your dreams come true.

**Embrace:** Calm; happy memories; yourself the way you are

**Avoid:** Going to extremes; dogmatic behavior; hypocrisy

**Also born on this day:** Oceanic explorer Jacques Cousteau; actors Peter Dinklage and Hugh Laurie; football coach Vince Lombardi; quarterback Joe Montana; actor/filmmaker Gene Wilder

# June 12 • Gemini

There are few people who have as many goals as those born on June 12. You want the very best that life can offer. You are a big thinker with the enthusiasm to go for broke. You see the big picture and have a great love of life. You are an incredible optimist and believe that everything that happens is for the best. When you must face a setback, you hold your head high and soldier on. You are a great self-starter and always seem to have a plan in mind. You have a genuine love of people and value diversity in your circle of pals.

**Embrace:** Advice; work ethic; sense of destiny

**Avoid:** Seeking out confrontation; poor choices; materialism

**Also born on this day:** Film director Irwin Allen; U.S. president George H. W. Bush; musician Pete Farndon; diarist Anne Frank; baseball player Hideki Matsui; singer/songwriter Robyn

# June 13 • Gemini

You are drawn to adventure and prefer living life on the edge. You have no patience with people who make only "safe" choices. You will always set your sights on what you want and go after it, no matter what it takes. You have a kinetic kind of charm that easily draws others to you. You do not usually follow your goals in a linear fashion; rather, you zig-zag back and forth, enjoying your progress toward your goal as much as the eventual destination.

**Embrace:** Self-expression; sentimentality; fame

**Avoid:** Feeling insecure; rage; feelings of guilt

**Also born on this day:** Comedian/actor Tim Allen; actors Chris Evans, Malcolm McDowell, and Stellan Skarsgård; poet William Butler Yeats

# June 14 • Gemini

You are in a class by yourself. You combine a winning personality with a penetrating intelligence that is truly disarming. You are a social gadfly and possess a great sense of your own importance. You are never shy about expressing your opinions. Nothing is out of bounds for people born on June 14. You want it all, and will bend all of your considerable efforts toward that end. You fear failure, yet you will put yourself out there in order to capture the brass ring.

**Embrace:** Decisiveness; organization; spirit of leadership

**Avoid:** Arrogance; self-doubt; being argumentative

**Also born on this day:** Photographer Margaret Bourke-White; singer/songwriter Boy George; tennis player Steffi Graf; revolutionary Che Guevara; author/abolitionist Harriet Beecher Stowe

# June 15 • Gemini

You know how to get your way with charm. Even though you're tough, you are never rude or abrasive. You possess the proverbial iron fist in a velvet glove. Even when you choose to play hardball with an opponent or rival, the individual in question may never realize they've been in a fight. You are a free-thinking, positive person with a strong can-do attitude. You work very hard to bring a goal to fruition, but you may not be willing to sacrifice your private life to achieve professional success. You understand that a happy personal life is more important than the achievement of career goals.

**Embrace:** Variety; focus; the joy of giving

**Avoid:** Playing favorites; indecisiveness; incompatibility

**Also born on this day:** Baseball player/manager Dusty Baker; actors Courtney Cox, Neil Patrick Harris, and Helen Hunt; singer Waylon Jennings

# June 16 • Gemini

Enthusiasm and a genuine curiosity about life mark your personality. You are one of life's true adventurers—to you, every day is a potential voyage of discovery. You have strong opinions yet are always open to new experiences. You have great people skills and possess the ability to rise to any social occasion. You are perceptive, bright, and as interested in those around you as in your own concerns. You enjoy spontaneity and are often reluctant to plot a course of action. You believe very much in the benevolence of time and enjoy taking each day as it comes.

**Embrace:** The wisdom of time; happy memories; being yourself

**Avoid:** Manipulative people; extreme thrills; bickering

**Also born on this day:** Apache leader Geronimo; comedian Stan Laurel; golfer Phil Mickelson; writer Joyce Carol Oates; rapper Tupac Shakur

# June 17 • Gemini

Unlike most Geminians, people born on this day are uncharacteristically serious. You are very concerned with being a success in life, yet a spirit of rebellion lurks behind your seemingly conservative and traditional surface. You have a vision all your own, but you aren't always sure just how to achieve it. You are concerned about stepping out of character and letting others see your vulnerabilities, and you have difficulty confiding your feelings to others. However, this is exactly what you need to do in order to come to grips with your true nature.

**Embrace:** Forgiveness; a joyous heart; attention to detail

**Avoid:** Excessive daydreaming; irresponsibility; ingratitude

**Also born on this day:** Artist M. C. Escher; singer Barry Manilow; composer Igor Stravinsky; tennis player Venus Williams

# June 18 • Gemini

You are a practical, sensible individual with far-reaching goals and endless ambition. It is very important to you to make a success of your life on every level. Although you understand the need for strong family ties and the fulfillment of personal happiness, you will sacrifice that happiness in order to put your plans into action. You aren't afraid of failure. You would rather lose on an opportunity by failing, than simply because you did not try. You keep busy and rarely have a moment of leisure at your disposal.

**Embrace:** Sensitivity; participation; inner path

**Avoid:** Ruthlessness; stubbornness; petulance

**Also born on this day:** Film critic Roger Ebert; singer/songwriter Paul McCartney; actors Richard Madden and Isabella Rossellini; country singer Blake Shelton

# June 19 • Gemini

You love being first in everything. You adore being in the spotlight and will fight to stay there. You are goal-oriented rather than egotistical; you know your own worth and are eager to prove it. You are an exuberant, creative person who seems to light up a room when you enter it. You have personality to spare and are not shy about displaying it. You have tremendous ambition and continually strive to improve yourself.

**Embrace:** Moments of solitude; autonomy; kismet

**Avoid:** Wallowing in sadness; selfishness; being easily discouraged

**Also born on this day:** Singer Paula Abdul; baseball star Lou Gehrig; comedian Moe Howard; film critic Pauline Kael; mathematician Blaise Pascal; novelist Salman Rushdie; actor Kathleen Turner

# June 20 • Gemini

You have a unique and interesting character. An attitude of emotional instability makes you very attractive to others; they may feel a need to "take care" of you, although you are actually much more centered than you appear. You want true happiness and will seek it out without fail. You have modest material needs, yet your spiritual and emotional needs are considerable. These are often achieved as you move along the path to self-discovery. You have a resoluteness about love that belies your casual nature.

**Embrace:** Mysticism; humor; beautiful thoughts

**Avoid:** Anger issues; unpredictable behavior; mood swings

**Also born on this day:** Actors Olympia Dukakis, John Goodman, and Nicole Kidman; playwright Lillian Hellman; singer Lionel Richie; film director Robert Rodriguez; singer/songwriter Brian Wilson

# CANCER

## June 21–July 22

Cancer is the fourth sign of the astrological year and is known by its astrological symbol, the Crab. Cancer individuals are intelligent, organized, and generous. With the moon as the planetary ruler, people born under this sign are considered to be home-loving and tenacious. They are devoted to family members and provide enormous emotional support.

**Element:** Water
**Planetary ruler:** Moon
**Key characteristic:** Emotion
**Strengths:** Intuitive; nurturing; maternal
**Challenges:** Controlling; bossy; manipulative

# June 21 • Cancer

People born on June 21 feel the need to do great good in the world. You are a happy individual with a genuine love for others. Fairness is a passion with you, and you have a personal need to live according to a set of ethical standards. You are talented and far-thinking, and your intelligence is combined with a great sense of caring. You do not shrink from becoming involved in situations that put your reputation on the line. You live large and dream large, always believing in your ability to make your goals come true.

**Embrace:** Sensuality; psychic awareness; a sense of history

**Avoid:** Pettiness; revenge; feelings of alienation

**Also born on this day:** Actors Juliette Lewis and Chris Pratt; Prince William, Duke of Cambridge; philosopher Jean-Paul Sartre; filmmaker Tony Scott

# June 22 • Cancer

You may be perceived as being sociable, but you are actually shy and seek your own company as much as possible. You are extremely sensitive to the emotional climate around you and can be both positively and negatively affected by it. You have a secret side, which you show only to those closest to you. Not given to displays of ego, you prefer to remain in the background, where you perform your daily responsibilities expertly and quietly. Your primary aim is to do as much good for others as possible. You are happiest when using your personal or professional influence in positive ways.

**Embrace:** Truth; understanding; your own limitations

**Avoid:** Deception; lecturing subordinates; feelings of superiority

**Also born on this day:** Author Dan Brown; politicians Dianne Feinstein and Elizabeth Warren; singer Cyndi Lauper; actor Meryl Streep; filmmaker Billy Wilder

# June 23 • Cancer

The people born on this date know how to have a good time. You are likely to be less serious and sensitive than most people born under the Cancer sign. You are generous, loyal, and have a heartfelt concern for others. You are an intelligent, commonsense type with an unexpected streak of eccentricity. You appreciate a funny story when you hear one and have a reputation for playing practical jokes on your closest friends and family members. You strive to achieve all that life can give you, and you continue to be thrilled and challenged by your future.

**Embrace:** Punctuality; logic; a sense of history

**Avoid:** Insensitivity; lack of humility; bossiness

**Also born on this day:** Researcher Alfred Kinsey; actor Frances McDormand; Olympian Wilma Rudolph; computer scientist Alan Turing; soccer player/manager Zinédine Zidane

# June 24 • Cancer

You have great personal charm, which may give others the impression that you are more mellow and less driven than you actually are. In fact, you are extremely career-oriented, and you've been known to sacrifice personal happiness in order to achieve your aims. You have a great need to break with tradition and the past. Creative and artistic, you feel you have something to prove to yourself and others, and you won't abandon that goal at any cost. You don't require a lot of attention for your efforts, only the knowledge that you have achieved a treasured goal.

**Embrace:** Probity; a sense of decorum; protective love

**Avoid:** Costly mistakes in love; economic stress; jealousy

**Also born on this day:** Musicians Jeff Beck and Mick Fleetwood; writer Ambrose Bierce; boxer Jack Dempsey; soccer star Lionel Messi

# June 25 • Cancer

You are unusually sensitive and apt to find yourself at odds with your true nature and the bold person you hope to be. You emit a dreamy and inexact persona, leading others to believe that you are not very focused. Actually, you are much more centered than you appear, although you can be distracted easily.

**Embrace:** Serenity; progress; self-discipline

**Avoid:** Risky choices; anger; petty limitations

**Also born on this day:** Illustrator Eric Carle; comedian Ricky Gervais; novelist George Orwell; singers George Michael and Carly Simon; Supreme Court Justice Sonia Sotomayor

# June 26 • Cancer

You are blessed with a brilliant, creative mind and a powerful personality that attracts others. You have extraordinary potential. Under your calm, quiet surface is a wicked sense of humor that can cut your scholarly reputation—and the pretensions of others—to ribbons. You wish to influence your world in a profound and meaningful way.

**Embrace:** Forgiveness; lasting love; integrity

**Avoid:** Insincerity; dwelling on heartache; useless wallowing

**Also born on this day:** Filmmaker Paul Thomas Anderson; author Pearl S. Buck; singer Ariana Grande; baseball star Derek Jeter; actor Chris O'Donnell; athlete Babe Didrikson Zaharias

# June 27 • Cancer

Although you possess a great sense of your own importance, you are not egotistical. You have a strong, imperious personality, yet you wear it with ease and grace. You exude a dynamic charm, which is unusual for Cancer natives, who are usually quiet and unassuming. You are upbeat, friendly, and devoted to creating meaningful friendships.

**Embrace:** Solace; religiosity; carefree spirit

**Avoid:** Envy; being disrespectful; self-pity

**Also born on this day:** Writer/producer/director J. J. Abrams; author/activist Helen Keller; actor Tobey Maguire; presidential candidate/businessman Ross Perot; fashion designer Vera Wang

# June 28 • Cancer

You have a marvelous sense of fun. This isn't just a sense of humor, but a way in which you choose to live life. If you can't have fun with a situation, you don't want to be involved in it. You are determined to wring every bit of humor out of even the most unlikely events. You are democratic in your attitude and can laugh at yourself. Although you are witty and hilarious, you are far from lighthearted at your core. You have very few close confidantes, yet you seldom open yourself up emotionally, even to those closest to you.

**Embrace:** Common sense; good nature; placidity

**Avoid:** Hasty actions; hurting others; deceit

**Also born on this day:** Actor Kathy Bates; actor/film director Mel Brooks; quarterback John Elway; King Henry VIII of England; entrepreneur Elon Musk; theologian John Wesley

# June 29 • Cancer

There is something almost preternaturally sensitive about people born on June 29. You are ruled more by emotion than reason, and you refuse to give up your idealism even in the face of hard facts and realism. Yet you are far more determined than your nature would make you seem. You have a great reservoir of faith and strength, which allows you to move forward despite trouble. You care about helping others. You are unselfish and always involved in some activity that brings hope or inspiration to others. You wish to perfect your creative talents, and believe in them, yet you often lack confidence in your ability to succeed.

**Embrace:** Time for yourself; rules; exhilaration

**Avoid:** Guilt; self-doubt; needy people

**Also born on this day:** Actor María Conchita Alonso; singers Nelson Eddy and Little Eva; film producer Robert Evans; comedian Richard Lewis

# June 30 • Cancer

You have an exceptionally well-balanced nature. You are materialistic, yet in a good sense because you wish to help others. At the same time, you'll never neglect the welfare of those closest to you. You are sensible, yet fun-loving. You strive for success, yet never lose sight of your personal commitments. You are strongly motivated to serve the greater good. You believe you can achieve whatever you want in life. This positive attitude is a self-fulfilling prophecy, because your dreams often come true. In the rare instances when one of your dreams is not realized, you have the resilience to adopt a philosophical attitude.

**Embrace:** Peace; ingenuity; love of humankind

**Avoid:** Being judgmental; greed; a sense of superiority

**Also born on this day:** Actor Susan Hayward; singer Lena Horne; swimmer Michael Phelps; boxer Mike Tyson

# July 1 • Cancer

Because you are naturally shy, you often prefer to work behind the scenes, letting others take the bows you are too timid to take. You are a wonderful humanitarian, and the gratification you receive by helping others is more valuable to you than any material consideration. You strive for perfection and have an unfortunate knack for being your own worst enemy. Even though you are good-hearted and generous, you seem to draw complications and controversy into your midst. You seem to have great emotional fragility, but your spirit is actually very strong.

**Embrace:** Structure; appearance; appeasement

**Avoid:** Self-criticism; self-consciousness; destructive habits

**Also born on this day:** Princess Diana; cosmetics company founder Estée Lauder; Olympian Carl Lewis; filmmaker Sydney Pollack; novelist George Sand; actor Liv Tyler

# July 2 • Cancer

You know how to use humor as both a tool and a weapon. You will always find a way to use your abilities to shine. You are self-analytical and go to great lengths to discover and understand your deepest inner drives. You believe in yourself and try to do the very best you can to live up to your potential.

**Embrace:** Spirituality; financial acumen; integrity

**Avoid:** Stinginess; lack of imagination; stubbornness

**Also born on this day:** Actor/comedian Larry David; novelist Hermann Hesse; Supreme Court Justice Thurgood Marshall; actor Margot Robbie

# July 3 • Cancer

Though you may seem conventional on the surface, you have a deeply mystical nature. You live life according to your own personal vision. At once eccentric and blessed with exceptionally good taste, you enjoy living the good life but never lose sight of your spiritual concerns. Although not especially goal-oriented, you are idealistic and eager to bring more good into the world.

**Embrace:** Social responsibility; tenacity; precision

**Avoid:** Intolerance; immaturity; lack of focus

**Also born on this day:** Actor Tom Cruise; novelist Franz Kafka; singer/actor Audra McDonald; playwright Tom Stoppard

# July 4 • Cancer

You are strong-willed and determined, dedicated to having your way, but you are also fair enough to admit when you are wrong. You have a humanitarian streak and will do many good deeds in your life, yet you prefer doing that work secretly. You take pleasure from starting each new day and realizing its potential.

**Embrace:** Discretion; reasonableness; emotional warmth

**Avoid:** Materialism; ingratitude; weak character

**Also born on this day:** U.S. president Calvin Coolidge; composer Stephen Foster; novelist Nathaniel Hawthorne; playwright Neil Simon; musician Bill Withers

# July 5 • Cancer

You need a large stage on which to live your life. You have a profound need to live in the "now," and yet you desire to transcend time through your own actions and plans. Intelligent, shrewd, and canny, you put your own stamp on events. You can talk yourself into almost any situation and impress others with your insightful thinking. Despite a strong cynical streak, your innate openness to others makes it easy for people to like you. You are ambitious but may not possess the self-discipline to see goals through to fruition.

**Embrace:** Gentle persuasion; acts of kindness; scruples

**Avoid:** Emotional depletion; self-pity; bluntness

**Also born on this day:** Circus owner P. T. Barnum; actor Edie Falco; musician Huey Lewis; politician Henry Cabot Lodge Jr.; soccer player Megan Rapinoe

# July 6 • Cancer

You have a great love of comfort and beauty. While status often plays a big role in your need to be surrounded by luxury, you are basically a down-to-earth person and derive a great deal of pleasure from being able to help those with fewer resources. You can be excessively demanding in your personal relationships. You don't like to share your friends with outsiders and may seem bossy when it comes to giving advice or suggestions. You seek your happiness and accomplishment through relationships with the people you love.

**Embrace:** Spiritual transcendence; charity; objectivity

**Avoid:** Pretense; snobbishness; always needing to win

**Also born on this day:** U.S. president George W. Bush; rock 'n' roll legend Bill Haley; painter Frida Kahlo; actors Janet Leigh and Sylvester Stallone

# July 7 • Cancer

People born on July 7 often feel the need to change the world they were born into. You are a visionary filled with artistic dreams, and the idea of being able to share your special talents with others holds great excitement for you. Dedicated to self-improvement in all its forms, you understand that the greatest lessons in life take place on a subconscious level. You have the potential for great spirituality but may spend a great deal of your life confused as to what you actually believe. You are not shy about letting others feel the influence of your own religious faith or spiritual conscience.

**Embrace:** Dedication to family; glamour; instinct

**Avoid:** Anger; guile; playing with people's feelings

**Also born on this day:** Artist Marc Chagall; comedian Jim Gaffigan; figure skater Michelle Kwan; baseball pitcher Satchel Paige; musician Ringo Starr

# July 8 • Cancer

Your quirky personality gives you a carefree, eccentric aspect, but in truth you are more serious-minded than you appear. You believe in conquering the "impossible dream" and have a strong need to display your abilities. Your idealistic streak is powerful, but you don't expect things to come to you easily. You understand that there must sometimes be a trade-off between what you want and what you can have. This is why the goals you set may be modest in contrast to your ambitions and abilities. You know the worth of personal goals, and you understand that money and possessions mean little unless loved ones are around to share these things.

**Embrace:** Moral character; spiritual energy; faith

**Avoid:** Prejudice; patronizing remarks; cheating

**Also born on this day:** Actors Kevin Bacon and Anjelica Huston; singer/actor Toby Keith; writer Anna Quindlen; oil industrialist John D. Rockefeller

# July 9 • Cancer

You are ambitious, positive, and eager to succeed. You will sacrifice a great deal of your time and effort in order to make your goals a reality. When you reach your goals, especially financial ones, you are invariably generous to those you love. Your natural leadership and bold and kinetic energy have a way of drawing friends easily. Your friends not only respect you, but often emulate you. You are a great role model. You have the ability to be happy with few material possessions, yet because you're willing to think more of others than yourself, you often receive blessings many times over.

**Embrace:** Fun; good fortune; a sense of the ridiculous

**Avoid:** Negativity; jealousy; controversial issues

**Also born on this day:** Actors Chris Cooper, Tom Hanks, and Jimmy Smits; mining magnate/philanthropist Daniel Guggenheim; artist David Hockney; inventor Elias Howe

# July 10 • Cancer

You are far more conventional than you appear. Although willful, you also possess considerable self-discipline. A natural authoritarian streak is balanced by your need to have the good opinion of others. You surround yourself with expensive possessions, yet it's not the things that dazzle you, but the realization that it has all been made possible by your hard work. You are talented in many respects, and do especially well in work that makes use of your wonderful organizational ability, as well as your effective management of other people's resources and abilities. You like to see tangible evidence of your efforts. For this reason, your goals are often material ones.

**Embrace:** Dynamic change; generosity; positive energy

**Avoid:** Manipulation; gossip; bad manners

**Also born on this day:** Tennis player Arthur Ashe; reformer/theologian John Calvin; novelist Marcel Proust; engineer/inventor Nikola Tesla; actor Sofia Vergara; artist James Whistler

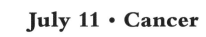

# July 11 • Cancer

Kind and generous, you use your extreme sensitivity to understand others; you are never victimized by your own finely tuned nature. You may not always appear to be on top of the world because your happy nature is something you often keep within yourself. Friends play an important part in your life. Self-sufficient, you nevertheless need to reach out to others. You are more concerned with how you feel about your life than how successful you are, or how much money you make. You need to feel emotionally involved in your work, and will never be happy with an unfulfilling job, even if it brings you a good living.

**Embrace:** Realism; encouragement; great expectations

**Avoid:** Excessive solitude; dwelling on unhappy memories; harmful associations

**Also born on this day:** U.S. president John Quincy Adams; fashion designer Giorgio Armani; actor Yul Brynner; writer E. B. White

# July 12 • Cancer

You are a partier who manages to retain a wholesome set of values and a strong humanitarian streak. An inner emotional pain encourages you to bring happiness to others. In this way, you're able to make yourself happy. You don't simply want to help others—you need to do so. You have a great need to connect with others on a profoundly emotional level. Even though you love material things, you understand the spiritual realm as well. You are energized by people and genuinely care for others, making friends wherever you go. People appreciate your tolerant viewpoint and appreciation and respect for the beliefs of others.

**Embrace:** Your own limitations; self-love; direction

**Avoid:** Cynicism; lack of focus; fair-weather friends

**Also born on this day:** Lyricist Oscar Hammerstein II; poet Pablo Neruda; writer Henry David Thoreau; figure skater Kristi Yamaguchi; activist Malala Yousafzai

# July 13 • Cancer

You are blessed with a charismatic personality that complements your gentle soul. Modest, you often receive far more attention than you are comfortable with. You have a fear of change, yet you understand that it is only through change that you are able to discover your own true nature. You have high ideals, and you are anxious to fulfill them. If you can influence others positively through your words or actions, you feel as if your fondest wish has come true. When you have a deeply personal goal, you are unlikely to share it with anyone else. You want very much to have a strong and stable personal life.

**Embrace:** Truth; mental toughness; sophistication

**Avoid:** Vacillation; foolish choices; allowing others' disapproval to discourage you

**Also born on this day:** Auto racer Alberto Ascari; film director Cameron Crowe; astrologer John Dee; actors Harrison Ford and Sir Patrick Stewart; playwright Wole Soyinka

# July 14 • Cancer

You are quick-witted, highly verbal, and prone to react in a haughty manner when crossed. You may seem very social and fun-loving, but you are considerably more serious than your personality makes you appear. You often make friends with professional associates who have profoundly and positively affected your life. You are dedicated to public expression of your opinions. Whether or not others believe in what you have to say is not really of any great concern to you. As long as you have a means to express yourself, you are content. If you do receive some measure of praise or acceptance for your beliefs, it's just frosting on the cake.

**Embrace:** Distinction; dedication to duty; acceptance

**Avoid:** Feelings of inferiority; inertia; doubts

**Also born on this day:** Writer/director Ingmar Bergman; U.S. president Gerald Ford; actors Matthew Fox and Jane Lynch; folk singer Woody Guthrie; animator William Hanna

# July 15 • Cancer

You often look to relationships to tell you who you are because you understand better than most people what the harmonics of day-to-day relationships signify if your life. You are sensitive, yet strong. You have a powerful attraction to beauty in all its aspects and seek to replicate it in your own life. Despite your charming personality, you are extremely sensitive and easily hurt. Getting along with others is your main goal, and although this talent comes naturally to you, it does not always come easily.

**Embrace:** Elegance; fearlessness; shared responsibilities

**Avoid:** Overwork; destructive behavior; grumpiness

**Also born on this day:** Author/columnist Arianna Huffington; football star/actor Alex Karras; novelist Iris Murdoch; painter Rembrandt; singer Linda Ronstadt; actors Brigitte Nielsen and Forest Whitaker

# July 16 • Cancer

You are very spiritual, with an innate sense of self. Although quiet, introspective, and seemingly shy, you have a strong will. You use the power of your positive attitude to get through tough times. You have a commonsense approach to life: You hope for the best but are never surprised when the opposite occurs. Material goals are rarely a strong focus for you. You are more concerned with expressing yourself creatively, connecting with loved ones on an emotional level, and making a difference in the lives of others.

**Embrace:** A joyful heart; fortitude; direction

**Avoid:** Isolation; lack of commitment; feeling blue

**Also born on this day:** Explorer Roald Amundsen; comedian/actor Will Ferrell; baseball star "Shoeless" Joe Jackson; football coach Jimmy Johnson; businessman Orville Redenbacher; actors Ginger Rogers and Barbara Stanwyck

# July 17 • Cancer

You are committed to excellence and achievement. You possess a high sense of honor and are a stickler for truth. Although you may have a decided weakness for flattery, you lack self-assurance and often hide behind a facade of sophistication. You have great emotional stamina and are very patient, understanding that you must wait your turn for success. You plan your achievements in a very organized and efficient way. You realize that even though long-range goals are important, you can't ignore the day-to-day details.

**Embrace:** Individuality; social skills; a happy disposition

**Avoid:** Procrastination; judging others; self-righteousness

**Also born on this day:** Comedian Phyllis Diller; writer Erle Stanley Gardner; U.S. naval hero John Paul Jones; actors James Cagney and Donald Sutherland; German chancellor Angela Merkel

# July 18 • Cancer

Gifted and unusual, you are a high-energy individual who understands the way karmic forces can facilitate self-realization. Deeply in touch with your own subconscious drives, you are usually able to achieve your aims through focusing on those inner desires. Your number-one goal is simply to "go for it." You get as much fun from participation as you do from victory. Although you have a competitive streak, it's competition itself—not the result—that turns you on.

**Embrace:** Irony; conviction; a dynamic spirit

**Avoid:** Fear of abandonment; bewilderment; self-blame

**Also born on this day:** Figure skaters Tenley Albright and Dick Button; business magnate Richard Branson; actors Kristen Bell and Vin Diesel; astronaut/U.S. senator John Glenn; South African president Nelson Mandela; writer Hunter S. Thompson; baseball executive Joe Torre

# July 19 • Cancer

People born on this date are quiet and inscrutable, with a deeply sensitive nature. You possess a generally sweet temperament and a true love of people; in return, you're easy to love. You don't try to grab the spotlight, though you may be thrust unwillingly into it because of a colorful accomplishment or dramatic heroism. You want to feel good about yourself, and you're usually able to achieve this by doing your best in everything you attempt and refusing to allow yourself to obsess over failure. You realize that everyone has challenges in life and that the difficult times lead to important learning opportunities.

**Embrace:** Vitality; self-worth; intelligent choices

**Avoid:** Belligerence; attitude problems; moodiness

**Also born on this day:** Actor Benedict Cumberbatch; painter Edgar Degas; guitarist Brian May; politician George McGovern

# July 20 • Cancer

You have an extremely strong sense of justice; integrity is everything to you. Although critical by nature, you never seem self-righteous. And although you love to get your own way, you understand the power and importance of compromise. You have a gentle yet determined nature. You possess a loving heart, and because of this you can see the positive side of any situation. You are an excellent friend with an extraordinary concern and sympathy for the people you love. You are extremely talented but are unlikely to realize your potential unless you have the approval and support of others.

**Embrace:** High ideals; sensitivity; a broad viewpoint

**Avoid:** Periods of depression; negative thoughts; feeling shy

**Also born on this day:** Model Gisele Bündchen; mountaineer Edmund Hillary; musician Carlos Santana; actors Sandra Oh and Natalie Wood

# July 21 • Cancer

You are torn between a need to be conventional and a desire to be original. You often use your larger-than-life personality to conceal your sense of insecurity. At the core of your being, you are extremely sensitive and may suffer much more than is apparent to others. Outwardly, you appear to believe in yourself and in your goals, yet a small core of doubt may reside deep in your heart. Although you may know intellectually that you have what it takes to succeed, emotionally you may be quite needy, requiring the validation of a friend or loved one.

**Embrace:** Acceptance; flamboyance; happy pastimes

**Avoid:** Destructive behavior; bad moods; fatalism

**Also born on this day:** Novelist Ernest Hemingway; baseball star C.C. Sabathia; lawyer Ken Starr; singer/songwriter Cat Stevens; actor/comedian Robin Williams

# July 22 • Cancer

You are a bold, active individual who goes to great lengths to prove your abilities, both to yourself and to others. Your edgy charm makes you appealing, yet your personality can be an acquired taste. You know how to impress others with very little effort. Your dreams are limitless. When you see the vast potential and opportunities open to you, you're challenged to go as far as your abilities will take you. You have old-fashioned values and believe that anything worth having is worth working hard to obtain.

**Embrace:** Career satisfaction; candor; true self

**Avoid:** Bias; gossip; being too critical of others

**Also born on this day:** Actors Willem Dafoe and Danny Glover; politician Bob Dole; singer/actor Selena Gomez; poet Emma Lazarus; fashion designer Oscar de la Renta; game show host Alex Trebek

# LEO

## July 23–August 22

Leo is the fifth sign of the astrological year and is known by its astrological symbol, the Lion. Leos are dynamic, self-confident, and highly dramatic. With the sun as the planetary ruler, people born under this sign are considered to be effective organizers, with an ability to lead and inspire others. They are talented individuals who find great happiness in self-expression.

**Element:** Fire
**Planetary ruler:** Sun
**Key characteristic:** Creativity
**Strengths:** Courage; integrity; confidence
**Challenges:** Egotism; selfishness; dominating to others

# July 23 • Leo

Like most Leos, you love being the center of attention. You have a pleasing personality and a good sense of humor. Even better, you love to tell jokes and use words in an unusual and memorable way. You do your homework: Whether working on a personal or a work-related project, you are always prepared. You're friendly and sociable, and you have the heart to transform a frivolous relationship into one that is deep and satisfying. You never stop working toward your goals. Although you may change direction, you start out waiting for that brass ring to come around, and when it does, you grab for it with enthusiasm.

**Embrace:** Constructive change; a happy heart; methodology

**Avoid:** Being too analytical; mental exhaustion; looking back

**Also born on this day:** Novelist Raymond Chandler; actors Woody Harrelson and Philip Seymour Hoffman; singer Alison Krauss

# July 24 • Leo

Despite having many natural talents and abilities, you are not without your problems. It's possible that early success may blind you to some of the pitfalls that await you. Optimism, unerring and eternal, is the keynote to your personality from childhood to old age. You're unwilling to acknowledge the possibility of failure, which is appropriate because you nearly always succeed. You have personality to spare and are often the center of attention among friends. You live in a benign universe where all the pieces of the cosmic puzzle eventually fall into place. Because of this, you're unlikely to approach your goals in a linear, organized fashion.

**Embrace:** Sensitivity; new ideas; commitment to excellence

**Avoid:** Instability; disrespect for authority and order; escapism

**Also born on this day:** Author Alexandre Dumas; aviator Amelia Earhart; poet Robert Graves; musician/actor Jennifer Lopez; actor Elisabeth Moss; pianist Peter Serkin

## July 25 • Leo

You are one of a kind—a true trailblazer. You have a bold attitude toward life, and you may seem overly ambitious to people who do not understand you. You have a fascinating brand of intelligence that is rooted in the subconscious and allows you to deal with people on many levels. Although you have the ability to reach the top with little effort, you can also be your own worst enemy; an inability to follow through on your aims can spell failure. With proper motivation, there's nothing you cannot achieve.

**Embrace:** Good deeds; sociability; progress

**Avoid:** Attitude problems; dishonesty; fear of failure

**Also born on this day:** Actors Estelle Getty and Barbara Harris; model Iman; football star Walter Payton

## July 26 • Leo

You have the genius to become an archetype in your field. It's not only that you possess amazing star quality and an intriguing personality, but you also have the ability to draw attention to yourself without trying to do so. You often find yourself at the center of controversy. You want very much to make a place for yourself in the world. You desire the material benefits that come with it, but more than that you want to enjoy the respect of your peers and colleagues. You will work tirelessly to achieve your goals.

**Embrace:** Stamina; inspiration; high ideals

**Avoid:** Boasting; manipulation of others; bad temper

**Also born on this day:** Figure skater Dorothy Hamill; musician Mick Jagger; filmmaker Stanley Kubrick; actor Helen Mirren; playwright George Bernard Shaw

# July 27 • Leo

You embody a duality that's not strictly evident except to those who know you well. You appear to be entirely at peace with your emotional landscape, yet you possess a spiritual core of steel that allows you to "soldier on" no matter what is arrayed against you.

**Embrace:** Emotional equilibrium; joy; living in the now

**Avoid:** Excessive impulsiveness; bad habits; isolation

**Also born on this day:** Baseball player/manager Leo Durocher; figure skater Peggy Fleming; baseball star Alex Rodriguez; golfer Jordan Spieth

# July 28 • Leo

You understand the value of your own singularity. Haughty yet lovable, you possess a personal code of ethics and a strong belief system. You have a great need to win, and you often hide your emotional vulnerability behind this showy aspect of your personality.

**Embrace:** Wisdom; fairness; family life

**Avoid:** Selfishness; greed; arrogance

**Also born on this day:** Suffragist Lucy Burns; cartoonist Jim Davis; artist Marcel Duchamp; First Lady Jacqueline Kennedy Onassis; author/illustrator Beatrix Potter

# July 29 • Leo

People born on this day are intensely focused. You like to be involved in all levels of every endeavor, and you are always willing to learn a little more about your world and the people in it. You are quite set in your ways and aren't likely to be swayed except by someone with exceptional skills of persuasion.

**Embrace:** Assimilation; strong opinions; culture

**Avoid:** Intolerant people; shyness; inattentiveness

**Also born on this day:** Musician Martina McBride; filmmaker Ken Burns; TV journalist Peter Jennings

# July 30 • Leo

You are creative in a spiritual and tangible sense. Your almost otherworldly nature is fortified by a strong sense of self. Although you occasionally seem aloof and distant, you have a great love for humanity and a genuine charisma that draws others to you. You possess a charm that sets you apart. Although you are a loner by preference and temperament, you are intensely devoted to your circle of friends. One of your major goals is to gather as much knowledge as you can. You have a great need to work with creative, exciting concepts.

**Embrace:** Mastering emotions; desire; self-esteem

**Avoid:** Fatalism; manipulation of others; intimidation

**Also born on this day:** Novelist Emily Brontë; industrialist Henry Ford; actors Laurence Fishburne and Hillary Swank; director Christopher Nolan; baseball legend Casey Stengel

# July 31 • Leo

You are a natural trendsetter who has the ability to sway others to your way of thinking. You are creative, friendly, and full of great ideas. You never play it safe; you put yourself out on a limb at every occasion to prove the worthiness of your positions. In more cases than not, your self-confidence and risk-taking are validated. You like diversity because it gives you the chance to discover fresh points of view. You have great enthusiasm for life. You're as excited about meeting personal goals in old age as you are when very young.

**Embrace:** Belief; goals; the strength to dream

**Avoid:** Willfulness; instability; foolish choices

**Also born on this day:** Business tycoon Mark Cuban; economist Milton Friedman; actor B. J. Novak; novelist J. K. Rowling

# August 1 • Leo

People born on August 1 have a lovable character and great potential. Your well-developed ego tells you just how special you are; you tend to set your sights very high and you occasionally come across as haughty. You want the validation of others, but you are not likely to sacrifice your true self to that aim. Once you set a goal for yourself, you doggedly pursue it. You have a real genius for creating interesting and fulfilling relationships that have positive effects on your life and the lives of the people closest to you.

**Embrace:** High energy; pragmatism; generosity

**Avoid:** Crass behavior; intolerance; poor personal choices

**Also born on this day:** Rapper Coolio; musician Jerry Garcia; designer Yves Saint Laurent; novelist Herman Melville; director Sam Mendes; actor Jason Momoa

# August 2 • Leo

You have an edgy, unique personality that makes you interesting to others. Like many Leos, you believe there is no such thing as having too many friends. Naturally, you enjoy being the center of attention, but because you dominate the spotlight in such a genteel and good-natured way, no one seems to mind. You see no barriers to making your goals come true. You want it all, and you have the chance to achieve your dreams if you keep your enthusiasm at a high pitch.

**Embrace:** Acts of charity; a happy disposition; imagination

**Avoid:** Antagonism; bad money habits; regrets

**Also born on this day:** Novelist James Baldwin; football player Billy Cannon; architect Pierre Charles L'Enfant; actors Myrna Loy and Peter O'Toole; baseball pitcher Tim Wakefield

# August 3 • Leo

You have star quality and are talkative and friendly. People born on August 3 are extremely ambitious. You work tirelessly toward your goals and do whatever you can to better yourself educationally and professionally. You possess great personal charm. Despite an appearance of self-absorption, you are deeply committed to causes that benefit others. Career success is a must for you, and it is to these ends that you are most likely to put your efforts. You may structure your potential goals from a very early age and attend to them with great care and self-discipline.

**Embrace:** Warmth; good advice; moderation

**Avoid:** Family discord; jealous friends; overindulgence

**Also born on this day:** Singer Tony Bennett; football star Tom Brady; designer Anne Klein; actor Martin Sheen; domestic diva Martha Stewart

# August 4 • Leo

You have considerable personal magnetism and an engaging personality. However, you are highly rebellious and may have a hard time fitting into a conventional mold. You prefer to do things your own way, even if this means hurting your chances for a promotion at work or receiving an accolade from friends. You have an unconventional view of what constitutes success. You don't look to achievements to make you feel good about yourself, nor do you expect to find satisfaction through worldly things. Instead, you're more concerned with living up to a strongly prescribed code of personal conduct.

**Embrace:** Quiet times; progress; sensitivity

**Avoid:** Rash decisions; empty promises; arrogance

**Also born on this day:** Musician Louis Armstrong; baseball star Roger Clemens; Meghan Markle, Duchess of Sussex; U.S. president Barack Obama; luggage maker Louis Vuitton

# August 5 • Leo

You are intelligent and witty, with a flair for good conversation and a fine sense of humor. You are generally good-natured and love to be around other people. However, you can be obsessively dogmatic about your ideas. You gravitate to jobs that let you indulge your passion for communication. You have incredibly high ideals, yet may not be sure just how to manifest them. Given your pride in your intellect and ideas, you have a great need to inspire others. Whether or not this is something you can meld into a career option, you can be depended upon to state your opinions and follow your convictions.

**Embrace:** The entrepreneurial spirit; praising others; love

**Avoid:** Egotism; forcing ideas on others; misjudging people

**Also born on this day:** Astronaut Neil Armstrong; basketball star Patrick Ewing; filmmaker John Huston; actor Maureen McCormick

# August 6 • Leo

You are even-tempered and pleasant. You have a talent for making friends, and you enjoy the social aspects of friendship but are more concerned with putting down emotional roots that will last a lifetime. You are exceptionally ambitious, and from an early age you felt the need to live up to your own potential. Although it may be hard for you to get your act together, once you set yourself a path you will follow it. You are constantly looking for a way to train your talents and bend yourself toward something important and interesting. Happiness and personal security are your major goals.

**Embrace:** Patience; identity; spiritual enlightenment

**Avoid:** Willfulness; putting demands on others; self-pity

**Also born on this day:** Comedian Lucille Ball; actor Robert Mitchum; basketball star David Robinson; poet Alfred, Lord Tennyson; artist Andy Warhol

# August 7 • Leo

You are mysterious and somewhat enigmatic. You like to make great mysteries of even the smallest things and refuse to live your life according to convention. You have a magnetic personality and an unabashed need to play mind games. Friendships can be rewarding for you as long as you feel comfortable enough with your pals to express your deepest feelings. Your dreams and goals can be as hard to define as you are. You are not usually materialistic, and therefore you tend to be most interested in goals that are spiritually oriented.

**Embrace:** Fairness; reality checks; authenticity

**Avoid:** Dark thoughts; revenge; selfish motives

**Also born on this day:** Countess/serial killer Elizabeth Báthory; American general Nathanael Greene; spy Mata Hari; actor Charlize Theron

# August 8 • Leo

You are a graduate of the proverbial school of hard knocks. Although you may seem unemotional or even distant, you are simply self-disciplined and in control of yourself. You are often forced to climb the hard road to success, but you wouldn't have it any other way. You want to earn every opportunity you receive and achieve success one step at a time; you look for no shortcuts. You are a great role model for your friends—by representing the marriage of talent and discipline, you are the envy of all who know you.

**Embrace:** Forgiveness; sensitivity; imagination

**Avoid:** Saying "I told you so"; a superior attitude; bitterness

**Also born on this day:** Tennis star Roger Federer; actor Dustin Hoffman; swimmer/actor Esther Williams

# August 9 • Leo

You are strong-minded, possessing the grit and ability to come back from difficult circumstances. You have a basic need to be challenged because it helps you to prove yourself on all levels of existence. Honor and integrity are important to you, and you won't bypass them for short-term gains. You have great personal dignity and carry yourself in a royal fashion. You are immaculate in your grooming habits and are always conscious of looking your best in any situation. You are extremely proud and may even seem vain, though your friends understand it's just a pose.

**Embrace:** Duty; continuity; spiritual transcendence

**Avoid:** Repetition; health risks; insecurity

**Also born on this day:** Basketball player Bob Cousey; singer Whitney Houston; hockey star Brett Hull; poet Philip Larkin; football/baseball star Deion Sanders

# August 10 • Leo

You are a study in contrasts. Although you have talents and resources that mark you as different, even unique, your greatest wish is to be a part of the crowd. You have leadership skills, and yet you know you have the best chance to achieve personal goals through group activities. Your goals change so often that you may have difficulty remembering just what it was you originally wanted. You gain your greatest satisfaction from your personal relationships, and have high hopes for the success and longevity of those unions.

**Embrace:** Productivity; aesthetics; idealism

**Avoid:** Underachievement; laziness; undue pride

**Also born on this day:** Actors Rosanna Arquette, Antonio Banderas, Norma Shearer, and Justin Theroux; U.S. president Herbert Hoover; British military leader William Howe; industrialist Henri Nestlé

# August 11 • Leo

You possess a great sense of curiosity about many aspects of life. You have an analytical intelligence that prompts you to wonder how things work. Often quiet and reserved, you may seem distant and aloof in your personal and professional relationships, yet you are actually sensitive and caring. You have amazing patience and rarely lose your temper or composure. People born on this date want to make a difference. You have a great capacity for kindness and care, which may draw you to the caring professions.

**Embrace:** Intuition; willingness to participate; charm

**Avoid:** Emotional walls; delays; being too practical

**Also born on this day:** Actors Viola Davis and Chris Hemsworth; writers Enid Blyton and Alex Haley; Apple co-founder Steve Wozniak

# August 12 • Leo

You require a great deal of personal freedom. You generally know exactly what you want out of life and don't know the meaning of the word quit. You go after your personal and professional aspirations with everything you've got. You also know how to bring out the best in others. People born on this day have great artistic potential. You have a very personal view of success, with goals directed more at process than product. You see your work as a pathway to a spiritual destination that cannot be accomplished through compromise of any sort.

**Embrace:** New horizons; persistence; details

**Avoid:** Stubbornness; self-importance; being defensive

**Also born on this day:** Filmmaker Cecil B. DeMille; musician Mark Knopfler; tennis star Pete Sampras

# August 13 • Leo

Eccentric and philosophical, you possess a kinetic energy that is the envy of all who know you. You have the ability to make a name for yourself in anything you attempt. Challenges seem to awaken your fighting spirit and give you the inspiration you need. Despite your loner mentality, you have a wide variety of friends. You seek friendship more for the satisfaction it gives you to observe human nature than for its emotional rewards. You want to live life on your own terms. You gravitate toward the unique, the strange, and the unusual.

**Embrace:** Adaptability; graciousness; mental quickness

**Avoid:** Holding grudges; a condescending attitude; immaturity

**Also born on this day:** Filmmaker Alfred Hitchcock; golfer Ben Hogan; sharpshooter Annie Oakley; suffragist Lucy Stone; economist Janet Yellen

# August 14 • Leo

Part mystery, part open book, you are perplexing, infuriating, and different. You usually manage to keep your true self carefully hidden from even your closest friends. This is a subtle defense mechanism that allows you to retain your autonomy without sacrificing the illusions held by others. Your charm effortlessly attracts people to you. Everyone will feel as if they know the "real" person, yet almost no one actually does. You do not rely on a succession of moves or a planned strategy to achieve your goals. You believe that fate, rather than effort, determines your future.

**Embrace:** The future; faith; nature's beauty

**Avoid:** Attempting to rewrite the past; lack of confidence; vengeful thoughts

**Also born on this day:** Actor Halle Berry; rocker David Crosby; basketball star Magic Johnson; comedian Steve Martin; novelist Danielle Steel

# August 15 • Leo

You have enormous leadership potential, and although you may seem egotistical, you are simply savvy about your own abilities. You are devoted to your friends. You feel you have many lessons to impart to others. You see the big picture better than almost anyone and yet can appreciate the value of details. You never limit your goals and are not afraid of failure. You don't allow yourself to see any impediment to your success. Although your level of ambition may seem awesome to some, those who know and understand you expect nothing less.

**Embrace:** Ceremony; fastidiousness; fair play

**Avoid:** Exhibiting a prickly personality; rudeness; dominating others

**Also born on this day:** Actor/filmmaker Ben Affleck; French emperor Napoleon Bonaparte; author Stieg Larsson; actor Jennifer Lawrence

# August 16 • Leo

You live your life with the volume turned up. You're dedicated and disciplined and have a strong sense of personal destiny. Although you absorb and listen to the criticism of others, it rarely causes you to change your game plan. You are quite concerned with your personal image and create a persona for yourself that is very much at odds with your true nature. It isn't characteristic for you to believe in luck—good, bad, or otherwise; you believe in making your own luck. You manage your goals on two separate levels: "dreaming" and "doing."

**Embrace:** Humility; good manners; stamina

**Avoid:** Stifling your true self; rudeness; a domineering attitude

**Also born on this day:** Actor Steve Carell; filmmaker James Cameron; baseball pitcher Yu Darvish; writer T. E. Lawrence; musician/actor Madonna

# August 17 • Leo

People born on August 17 possess enormous spiritual power. You are highly focused and always follow your own path; you're seldom influenced by trends. Although personable, you have an aloof quality. You appear steady and unflappable to others, but there are times when emotions get the better of you and your logic is useless. You have a sincere commitment to making your dreams come true. You are extremely disciplined and can call upon great reserves of emotional and spiritual energy to sustain you during your climb to the top. You have very little interest in fame and fortune.

**Embrace:** Originality; technology; free expression of emotions

**Avoid:** Brooding; anger; a bad attitude

**Also born on this day:** Frontiersman Davy Crockett; actors Robert De Niro, Sean Penn, and Mae West

# August 18 • Leo

You have a penchant for taking chances and get a thrill out of living dangerously. You have no hidden agenda—you know what you want and don't try to hide the fact. Your boldness is part of your attractiveness, which is heightened by your natural charm. People born on this day are eternally optimistic, possessing great mental and physical endurance. You believe in yourself and know you have the grit and determination to make your mark. Even if a dream proves to be unrealistic or unreachable, you will continue doing everything you can to bring a dream to fruition.

**Embrace:** Selectivity; exuberance; scruples

**Avoid:** Foolish risks; confrontation; irresponsibility

**Also born on this day:** Baseball star Roberto Clemente; actors Robert Redford and Shelley Winters; journalist Bob Woodruff

# August 19 • Leo

You have big dreams and enjoy pushing yourself to the limit, both physically and mentally. You may have some awkward years before you decide how to focus your energies, but once you put it all together there is no stopping you. Egotism can occasionally get in the way of your common sense. Your greatest talent is your ability to adapt. You will work ceaselessly toward goals. Once you achieve your dreams, you may be at a loss to find something to replace them.

**Embrace:** Restraint; sincerity; original vision

**Avoid:** Temper tantrums; mood swings; petulance

**Also born on this day:** Fashion designer Coco Chanel; U.S. president Bill Clinton; publisher Malcolm Forbes; writer Ring Lardner Jr.; aviator Orville Wright

# August 20 • Leo

Although you are outwardly affable and genuinely sweet, you also have a dark side. You like keeping secrets, even from those closest to you. This stems from the need to be self-protective. You are extremely sensitive, and you inevitably feel the disappointments and sadness of loved ones as keenly as you feel your own. You have great determination and the will to succeed. As long as you retain these gifts you can look forward to the success you deserve.

**Embrace:** Education; generosity; optimism

**Avoid:** Alienation; coldness; inability to compromise

**Also born on this day:** Actors Amy Adams and Joan Allen; musician Isaac Hayes; U.S. president Benjamin Harrison; rocker Robert Plant; novelist Jacqueline Susann

# August 21 • Leo

You have the need to live large. You are a practitioner of conspicuous consumption, and you don't make any apologies about it. You are jovial and friendly, with a winning personality that endears you to others. You have a great love and respect for learning. You like to be in the center of things. You prefer a demanding job that keeps you going at a hectic pace all day long. People born on August 21 have unflappable optimism.

**Embrace:** Scholarship; rules; psychic awareness

**Avoid:** Bragging; selfishness; questionable advice from others

**Also born on this day:** Bandleader Count Basie; sprinter Usain Bolt; Google co-founder Sergey Brin; sportscaster Jack Buck; actor Kim Cattrall; basketball star Wilt Chamberlain; musician Kenny Rogers

# August 22 • Leo

You have personal charm and plenty of class. High-strung and somewhat nervous, you thrive on attention from others. Before you can reach your goals, you need to learn to believe in yourself. You are extremely modest. It often takes the personal validation of a close friend, family member, or colleague to make you recognize your own talents and abilities. For this reason, you can benefit from a mentor. You don't make friends easily, but are intensely loyal to those you have.

**Embrace:** Good attitude; belief in nature; stamina

**Avoid:** Heeding inner fears; pettiness; moodiness

**Also born on this day:** Novelist Ray Bradbury; musician John Lee Hooker; NFL coach Bill Parcells; writer Dorothy Parker; baseball player Carl Yastrzemski

# VIRGO

## August 23–September 22

Virgo is the sixth sign of the astrological year and is known by its astrological symbol, the Virgin. Virgo individuals are intelligent, patient, and humble. With Mercury as the ruling planet, people born under this sign are considered to be quick-thinking, observant, and analytical. They possess an organized mind and have the logic to solve even the most difficult problems.

**Element:** Earth
**Planetary ruler:** Mercury
**Key characteristic:** Detail-oriented
**Strengths:** Precise; orderly; efficient
**Challenges:** Nervous; sarcastic; overcritical

# August 23 • Virgo

You are a guileless, genuinely nice person with a mercurial, kinetic charm that brings you great affection from others—and it doesn't hurt that you're constantly looking after other people's happiness and welfare. Your graceful bearing combines with a light touch of sophistication. You achieve your goals in an orderly, practical manner. You learn from every experience and use those lessons to your own best advantage in future situations. Because of your enthusiastic nature, you never lose faith in your own ability to make things happen. If your goals are sidetracked, you look at it as a chance to regroup rather than as a misfortune.

**Embrace:** Emotional depth; self-assurance; nobleness

**Avoid:** Stubbornness; stress; burning the candle at both ends

**Also born on this day:** Basketball star Kobe Bryant; actor/dancer Gene Kelly; actors Shelley Long and Vera Miles; drummer Keith Moon

# August 24 • Virgo

You are a real lady or gentleman. You are known for your excellent manners, good disposition, and the generosity you display to those closest to you. Your greatest challenge is remembering to be yourself. Because you may not have a lot of confidence in your abilities, you often look to colleagues or friends for validation. Your innate shyness makes it hard for you to put yourself "out there," but with the encouragement of good friends, you're more likely to give it a try. You are a doer, and you will never stop trying to achieve your dreams. Once you learn to trust your own instincts, you can go far.

**Embrace:** Inner drives; communication; sensuality

**Avoid:** Belligerence; selfish motives; pettiness

**Also born on this day:** Comedian Dave Chappelle; filmmaker Ava DuVernay; actor/comedian/writer Stephen Fry; actor Marlee Matlin; baseball star Cal Ripken Jr.

# August 25 • Virgo

You have a complicated nature. On one hand, you seem to derive a great deal of emotional sustenance from the approval of those close to you. Yet you also qualify as a true pioneer who is not afraid to accept the personal and professional challenges that come your way. When you find your niche, you make bold strides in whatever you attempt. Although you may have worldly goals early in life, you will almost certainly turn toward a spiritual path sooner or later. You are intrigued by life's mysteries, and want to know and understand your own motivations and those of others.

**Embrace:** A positive self-image; happy memories; learning

**Avoid:** Being weighed down by regret; finding fault; worrying

**Also born on this day:** Composer/conductor Leonard Bernstein; director Tim Burton; actor Sean Connery; singer Billy Ray Cyrus; tennis star Althea Gibson

# August 26 • Virgo

Quiet and introspective, you possess a strong sense of purpose. You have a great devotion to fairness and a desire to apply your energies for the benefit of others. You don't make a show of yourself in any way, and you prefer that others not attempt to put you in the spotlight. You aren't as concerned with success as you are with getting things done the best way you can. You aren't competitive and prefer to take the middle road in your approach to most of life's challenges. You are a careful planner, who takes one step at a time toward making a dream come true.

**Embrace:** Solidarity; passion; impossible odds

**Avoid:** Transitory relationships; worry; prejudice

**Also born on this day:** Journalist Ben Bradlee; politician Geraldine Ferraro; novelist/playwright Zona Gale; musician Branford Marsalis; missionary Mother Teresa

# August 27 • Virgo

You are practical and use your creative abilities to advertise a particular point of view. You feel all of your responsibilities deeply. You have a social conscience and often involve yourself in useful projects that teach or otherwise help others. Bold and determined, you have a hard time taking orders from others. You steer your own course and take responsibility for your own mistakes. Because you strive for self-sufficiency, you would rather have fewer material possessions and be your own boss than have a great deal and be in hock to others.

**Embrace:** Forgiveness; a sense of humor; integrity

**Avoid:** Grudges; a wounded heart; jealousy

**Also born on this day:** Fashion designer Tom Ford; U.S. president Lyndon Baines Johnson; comedian Pee-wee Herman (Paul Reubens); actors Barbara Bach, Aaron Paul, and Chandra Wilson

# August 28 • Virgo

You have a strongly creative nature that needs to be addressed. You grasp the interdependence of nature and art—you have a sensitive side that's complemented by inner strength, which helps you deal with life's demanding challenges. You have a good self-image and plenty of self-confidence, but you can be deeply hurt by others' bad opinion of you. Your biggest strength is your ability to know what you really want out of life, and you are never satisfied with just "getting by." You want to improve your mind, body, and soul in every aspect of life.

**Embrace:** A positive self-image; lasting love; decency

**Avoid:** Pretentiousness; cynicism; indifference

**Also born on this day:** Comedian/actor Jack Black; writer/philosopher Johann Wolfgang von Goethe; figure skater Scott Hamilton; comic book artist Jack Kirby; musician Shania Twain

# August 29 • Virgo

You have a strong life force that's keenly expressed through your emotions. You have the potential to lead an extraordinarily spiritual life, though you must come to grips with all aspects of your personal relationships before this can be accomplished. You need to follow your own path, and you will experience setbacks and disappointment if you allow yourself to be influenced against your better judgment. You are not very adventurous, and you are likely to befriend individuals who are very much like you. Because you are so emotional, you experience profound joy and sadness in romance.

**Embrace:** Clarity; balance; emotional transcendence

**Avoid:** Insecurity; self-criticism; compliance

**Also born on this day:** Director/actor Richard Attenborough; actor Ingrid Bergman; musician Michael Jackson; philosopher John Locke; politician/war hero John McCain

# August 30 • Virgo

People born on August 30 tend to have such a positive attitude about life that setbacks and delays don't slow them down. You have a high level of self-confidence and can envision your success even before it happens. You have an overwhelming urge to express your individual identity, and you are known for your discriminating good taste. You have a great love of learning, travel, and the written word. Although you seem calm on the surface, you're actually high-strung and excitable. You're extremely fun-loving and enjoy a vibrant social life. You are a sincere friend and like to spend time with good pals.

**Embrace:** Self-esteem; expectations; an open mind

**Avoid:** Ego issues; self-criticism; compliance

**Also born on this day:** Investor Warren Buffett; cartoonist Robert Crumb; actor Cameron Diaz; novelist Mary Shelley; baseball star Ted Williams

# August 31 • Virgo

You have a showy yet tasteful personality, and you bask in the loving approval of others. Although you are original and intelligent, you are often impractical. Your eclectic tastes display erudition. You often find yourself in unusual circumstances; this suits your love of adventure. You show your unique nature through the friends you make. You may not think of yourself as especially goal-oriented, but you go after things in a big way—but often without making the necessary plans or considering details. You are able to see things from a wide perspective and to appreciate eccentricity and inventiveness.

**Embrace:** Organizational skills; centeredness; high spirits

**Avoid:** Confusion; domestic upheavals; hasty actions

**Also born on this day:** Educator/civil rights activist Marva Collins; actor Richard Gere; educator Maria Montessori; musician Van Morrison

# September 1 • Virgo

You have a practical approach to life that enables you to get things done. You take great pride in your ability to organize your activities, and although you keep up a steady pace with every project, you never hurry. You do the best you can, every day, on every project, without exception. To you, honest effort equals success. You believe in making use of your best capabilities and will never sacrifice your own security or that of your loved ones to try something wild or unprovable.

**Embrace:** Freedom; liberality; a sense of humor

**Avoid:** Overwork; being too serious; solitude

**Also born on this day:** Novelist Edgar Rice Burroughs; singers Gloria Estefan and Barry Gibb; boxer Rocky Marciano; comedian/actor Lily Tomlin

# September 2 • Virgo

You need to feel that you're in control in all aspects of life. You are practical, serene, organized, and have great leadership potential. You are devoted to your loved ones. You can always see the humor in things, though you don't often show that side of yourself to the world. You tend to keep your goals to yourself—not because you don't believe in yourself, but rather because you fear letting others down if you fail to achieve what you set out to do. Yet quietly, without ceremony, you do reach your ultimate objectives.

**Embrace:** Self-sufficiency; high spirits; spontaneity

**Avoid:** Bad habits; lack of focus; repeating the same mistakes in love

**Also born on this day:** Football player/announcer Terry Bradshaw; boxer Lennox Lewis; actors Salma Hayek and Keanu Reeves

# September 3 • Virgo

Highly ambitious and incredibly goal-oriented, you may be fortunate enough to achieve your ultimate goals early in life. You don't believe in limitations and will pursue your dreams with every bit of energy and vitality you possess. You have a great capacity for spirituality, yet this side of your nature may not come to the surface until later in life. You may seem materialistic to others, but that's only outward evidence of your natural practicality. You have a strong entrepreneurial spirit and are always looking for ways to break out on your own.

**Embrace:** Family values; good times; domesticity

**Avoid:** Loneliness; predictability; boredom

**Also born on this day:** Musician Al Jardine; novelist Alison Lurie; snowboarder Shaun White; actor Charlie Sheen

# September 4 • Virgo

Unique and independent-minded, you march to the beat of a different drummer. You often display extraordinary bravery in the simple act of living your life. You want to know the truth about yourself, whether positive or negative. Even though you have a great deal of common sense, you are also a natural risk-taker. Every day seems to beckon to you with new dreams and new goals. You never stop being excited by life and all its myriad experiences. You have a strong curiosity about everything that surrounds you, and you will continue to look for answers as long as you live.

**Embrace:** Cooperation; young ideas; commitment

**Avoid:** Fixation; obsessive love; incompatibility

**Also born on this day:** Radio broadcaster Paul Harvey; singer Beyoncé Knowles; novelist Richard Wright

# September 5 • Virgo

You stand out in a crowd. Intelligent and composed, you are usually in control of your emotions, no matter how severe your circumstances may be. Relationships are the very essence of life for you, and you spend your entire life working to make them the best they can be. Friends have a way of becoming family, while family members become true friends. Although you may satisfy yourself after attaining modest goals, it's not because you can't appreciate the big picture. Rather, it defines your notion that everything you put your hand to must be treated with equal conscientiousness and respect.

**Embrace:** Your muse; special occasions; individuality

**Avoid:** Dependence; irrationality; mood swings

**Also born on this day:** Outlaw Jesse James; singer/songwriter Freddie Mercury; comedian/actor Bob Newhart; actors Michael Keaton and Raquel Welch

# September 6 • Virgo

You live life on the edge. You are not concerned for your physical safety and don't hesitate to take chances, including—sometimes—foolish ones. You have a strong spirit and a gentle nature, along with a great love for beauty in all its forms. You incorporate that characteristic into your life, work, and relationships. Style, art, and all things beautiful speak to you in a language few people understand. Self-discipline is not your greatest strength, and some of your goals may have to wait until you can learn to become more organized and aggressive.

**Embrace:** Respect; inner voice; career achievement

**Avoid:** Indecisiveness; impatience; emotional neediness

**Also born on this day:** Activist Jane Addams; actors Jane Curtin and Idris Elba; French aristocrat Marquis de Lafayette; musician Roger Waters

# September 7• Virgo

Although you may seem docile on the surface, you have a volatile inner energy that you use in pursuit of achievement. You are extremely ambitious, yet never ruthless. You believe in playing by the rules and will not change your attitude no matter how badly you want success. You may seem to clamor for your place in the spotlight, but you prefer security to unpredictable excitement. Because you are typically a loner, you don't make friends easily. Your shyness may make you appear snobbish or aloof, though you are actually in great need of finding people who understand you.

**Embrace:** Sensitivity; good intentions; a crusading spirit

**Avoid:** Single-mindedness; self-praise; anger

**Also born on this day:** Musician Buddy Holly; filmmaker Elia Kazan; painter Grandma Moses

# September 8 • Virgo

You are an inveterate searcher of truth. You may come to the deepest realization of self after suffering a great emotional pain or disappointment. You are determined to get to the heart of things. Your practical view of life allows you to withstand difficulties without losing faith in yourself or your objectives. Friendship means a great deal to people born on this date. You feel a need to cultivate close relationships with people who share your values and beliefs, and may have a hard time connecting with those who see life differently than you do.

**Embrace:** Identity; loyalty; inner path

**Avoid:** Feelings of betrayal; destructive thoughts; brooding

**Also born on this day:** Musician Patsy Cline; singer Pink; politician Bernie Sanders; actor Peter Sellers

# September 9 • Virgo

You are a perfectionist—a fact that often makes your own life difficult while infuriating everyone around you. You put incredible pressure on yourself, not so much to succeed but rather to be the best in your own eyes. People born on September 9 are doers and achievers. You don't wait for opportunity to knock on your proverbial door—you go out and seize it. However, you need to learn to slow down and enjoy your success. Your goals should be spiritual as well as material.

**Embrace:** Virtue; calm; a nurturing spirit

**Avoid:** Bickering; scheming; undeserved pride

**Also born on this day:** Soccer player Luka Modrić; musician Otis Redding; comedian/actor Adam Sandler; novelist Leo Tolstoy; actors Hugh Grant and Michelle Williams

# September 10 • Virgo

You have unique magnetism and a winning personality that make you incredibly appealing to others. You are able to project your inner self through your personality. You prize the intangibles of life, such as relationships, integrity, and learning. You may not have clearly defined goals. The trip to your destination is likely to interest you more than the destination itself. Once you find a goal that enthralls you, you give it your all. You give new meaning to the word "enthusiasm."

**Embrace:** True motives; authenticity; psychic sensitivity

**Avoid:** Fear of change; making demands; irrational choices

**Also born on this day:** Ballerina Misty Copeland; actor Colin Firth; fashion designer Karl Lagerfeld; baseball player Roger Maris; golfer Arnold Palmer

# September 11 • Virgo

Although you may seem excessively emotional, you're actually very centered and you know exactly what you wish to accomplish in life. Because your belief in yourself is strong and unwavering, you are able to withstand criticism. You possess an extraordinary sense of loyalty toward your friends, and you will go to extremes in order to make your loved ones happy and secure. You know you must make sacrifices in order to make certain dreams come true, yet you never put your goals ahead of the people who are important to you.

**Embrace:** Artistic expression; a generous heart; positive energy

**Avoid:** Temptations; ambition; dependence

**Also born on this day:** Filmmaker Brian DePalma; football coach Tom Landry; writer D. H. Lawrence

# September 12 • Virgo

You are much more jovial and relaxed than the typical Virgo. You are naturally happy and habitually look on the bright side. Nothing gets you down for long. You seek to put your resources to work helping others. Whether you possess a great deal of material wealth or not, you always find a way to give something to an individual who has less. Friends are one of the most important factors in your life. You draw a great deal of inspiration from your pals, and may in turn serve as a counselor or confidante.

**Embrace:** Originality; imaginative people; accountability

**Avoid:** Showing off; need for constant approval; personal fulfillment at the expense of others

**Also born on this day:** Musician/actor Jennifer Hudson; Olympian Jesse Owens; singer Barry White

# September 13 • Virgo

You do not typify the usual Virgo traits of caution and conservatism; you're more likely to walk on the wild side. You are a style setter in your own way. You have a cool and collected attitude that marks you as a winner. Your ability to make others feel comfortable and confident in any social situation is indicative of your natural talent as a host or hostess. A loner by temperament, you try to surround yourself with quirky, interesting people. You prize independence, originality, and the ability to be yourself in any situation.

**Embrace:** Irony; high energy; personal choice

**Avoid:** Conceit; envy; being overly sensitive

**Also born on this day:** Actor Claudette Colbert; author Roald Dahl; chocolate tycoon Milton S. Hershey; filmmakers Bong Joon-ho and Tyler Perry

# September 14 • Virgo

You embody the true spirit of Virgo perfectionism and criticism. You have extraordinarily high standards and refuse to settle for second-best. Complex and seemingly demanding, you can be difficult to live with, but no one can doubt your sincerity. You have a humanitarian streak and want to make an important contribution to society. You aspire to perfection and feel insecure about your efforts if you fall short of that mark. One of your goals is to harmonically balance the professional and personal sides of your life.

**Embrace:** Ambition; a crusading spirit; vitality

**Avoid:** Stubbornness; fear of commitment; stress

**Also born on this day:** Actor Clayton Moore; activist Margaret Sanger; musician Amy Winehouse

# September 15 • Virgo

You have a natural talent for communicating with others. You are scrupulously truthful, yet you need to find a personal dream world that allows you an escape from the harshness of reality. You have a sensitive nature that may at times be obscured by your sparkling personality. People born on this date are immensely talented, usually in an artistic way. You enjoy being in the spotlight and may chase that dream early in life. Once you start making a place for yourself in the world, however, you begin to prioritize spiritual goals. To understand your deepest motivations, you must explore your inner landscape.

**Embrace:** Vitality; focus; emotional security

**Avoid:** Inflexibility; being judgmental; pleasure-seeking

**Also born on this day:** Novelist Agatha Christie; Prince Harry, Duke of Sussex; actor Tommy Lee Jones; filmmaker Oliver Stone

# September 16 • Virgo

You have a deeply spiritual nature that sustains you in times of trouble and confusion. Although you tend to be very "together," you may seem vulnerable, even fragile, on the outside. People born on this date are often deeply religious. You can never be happy in a profession that brings money and nothing else. You need to feel as if your work contributes something valuable to yourself and to others. For this reason, you may choose a caring profession. You are not generally competitive, preferring to score a personal best rather than a victory over someone else.

**Embrace:** Intuition; imagination; determination to succeed

**Avoid:** Instability; unrequited love; solitude

**Also born on this day:** Actors Lauren Bacall and Peter Falk; magician David Copperfield; blues musician B. B. King

# September 17 • Virgo

You are a fighter and a survivor who doesn't understand the concept of giving up. You take life very seriously, approaching each obstacle in your path as a challenge. You are loyal and steadfast, and expect friends to be the same way. You have real grit and remain true to your ideals no matter what. You like being in charge. This isn't a power trip, but merely an invocation of your best qualities. You have a quiet, reassuring presence that's helpful in giving those under you a sense of confidence.

**Embrace:** Good examples; understanding; spiritual riches

**Avoid:** Possessiveness; superficial relationships; fatalism

**Also born on this day:** Actor Anne Bancroft; basketball player/coach Phil Jackson; singer/songwriter Hank Williams

# September 18 • Virgo

You have great self-control and an ability to use your energies for valuable achievement. You are dedicated to self-sufficiency and don't like to rely on others. You are serious and mysterious, going about your life with quiet precision. You have an inability to trust all but those closest to you, and may discreetly promote yourself as enigmatic, even eccentric. You prefer to keep your own counsel, yet when you discover someone you can trust, you're immensely grateful to have a confidante. You understand how to put all of your resources into getting what you want out of life.

**Embrace:** Emotional equilibrium; a love of nature; laughter

**Avoid:** Passivity; deception; secrecy

**Also born on this day:** Physicist Jean Bernard Léon Foucault; actors James Gandolfini and Greta Garbo

# September 19 • Virgo

Few people possess your charming personality and physical elegance. You always take great care in how you present yourself, both physically and in the general tenor of your actions, so that what people see is a sleek and refined package. Although you like being the center of attention, you can never be called an egotist. You are a lifelong student who never loses interest in the mystery and beauty of life. If you can overcome your vulnerabilities, you can accomplish anything you wish. Your ability to believe in yourself is the key factor.

**Embrace:** Excellence; innocence; a generous spirit

**Avoid:** Aloofness; isolation; excessive practicality

**Also born on this day:** Comedian/TV host Jimmy Fallon; novelist William Golding; baseball player/broadcaster Joe Morgan; actors Jeremy Irons and Adam West

# September 20 • Virgo

You are the ultimate professional in all you do. Practical and organized, you participate actively in life. You are a doer, not a watcher. You are so frank and earnest about achieving your desires that you may appear to be opportunistic, but you're just being honest about your feelings.

**Embrace:** Education; recognition; questioning authority

**Avoid:** Blunt speech; emotional bullying; disapproval

**Also born on this day:** Basketball coach Red Auerbach; hockey star Guy Lafleur; actor Sophia Loren; writer Upton Sinclair

# September 21 • Virgo

You are quiet and personable. You have a tremendous fear of failure, and for this reason you may sometimes hold back your enthusiasm and commitment. The ability to cross that divide is a real stretch for you, but when you make it you empower yourself as never before.

**Embrace:** Spiritual fulfillment; ethics; modesty

**Avoid:** Procrastination; easy answers; self-indulgence

**Also born on this day:** Musicians Leonard Cohen and Faith Hill; actor/comedian Bill Murray; writers Stephen King and H. G. Wells

# September 22 • Virgo

You have a powerful personality that exerts considerable influence over others. Although you may be drawn to scholarly pursuits, you almost always find yourself in demand to fulfill more worldly aims. You like to be at the center of activity.

**Embrace:** Graciousness; setting an example; knowledge

**Avoid:** Shiftlessness; abandonment issues; a need for validation

**Also born on this day:** Singer Andrea Bocelli; baseball manager Tommy Lasorda; novelist Fay Weldon

# LIBRA

## September 23–October 22

Libra is the seventh sign of the astrological year and is known by its astrological symbol, the Scales. Libra individuals are artistic, affectionate, and refined. With Venus as the ruling planet, people born under this sign are considered to be attractive and fashion-conscious. They seek peace and joy through personal and professional relationships.

Element: Air
Planetary ruler: Venus
Key characteristic: Harmony
Strengths: Diplomacy; charm; love of beauty
Challenges: Indecision; narcissism; superficiality

# September 23 • Libra

Individuals born on this date combine a love of learning with excellent good taste—the hallmark of the Libra sign. You are an energetic fact-finder who tirelessly seeks answers to life's difficult questions. You have a friendly, outgoing disposition that commands the love and respect of others, and you manage to project an image of seriousness while still maintaining your personal charm. Although others may think you are indecisive, it is simply your nature to weigh all aspects of a question before deciding. Not only do you possess a wonderful sense of social decorum, you also cultivate deeply satisfying friendships.

**Embrace:** Permanence; stability; attention to detail

**Avoid:** Irresponsibility; arguments; mental exhaustion

**Also born on this day:** Musicians Ray Charles, John Coltrane, and Bruce Springsteen; comedian Hasan Minhaj; sculptor Louise Nevelson; activist Victoria Woodhull

# September 24 • Libra

People born on this day are dynamic, artistic, and luxury-loving. Possessed of a charming personality and a subtle intelligence, you are far more complicated than you seem to be. Although your professional achievements give you a great deal of emotional fulfillment, you experience most of your satisfaction—and a great deal of your pain—from your personal relationships. In order to achieve the goals you set for yourself, you must bring your common sense into line with your intelligence. You want the world to value your talents, yet before this can happen you must become accountable to yourself.

**Embrace:** Family values; personal excellence; truth

**Avoid:** Restlessness; appeasement; dissatisfaction

**Also born on this day:** Novelist F. Scott Fitzgerald; football star "Mean Joe" Greene; puppeteer Jim Henson

# September 25 • Libra

You have a strong sense of personal honor and integrity. You are sharply focused and expect a great deal of yourself. Opinionated and ethical, you are highly motivated to achieve success on both worldly and spiritual levels. And then there's a dark side that few people glimpse—that is, your tendency to brood. You favor a small but select circle of friends and aren't given to confiding in others. Although you are interested in exploring the full spectrum of your own nature, this can be difficult for you because you are sometimes afraid of your own intensity.

**Embrace:** Satisfaction; self-determination; progress

**Avoid:** Limitations; complicated relationships; brooding

**Also born on this day:** Novelist William Faulkner; baseball player/ sportscaster Phil Rizzuto; writer Shel Silverstein; basketball player Scottie Pippen; actors Michael Douglas, Donald Glover, Catherine Zeta-Jones, and Will Smith; journalist Barbara Walters

# September 26 • Libra

You are a study in contrasts and contradictions. You possess a sympathetic nature yet have a strong will. Self-disciplined and practical, you are also extremely romantic and given to periodic flights of fancy. Although you appear reserved, you have a wonderful sense of humor that can diffuse any problem or touchy situation. You are a self-starter who can set a task for yourself and rely on the results. Goal-oriented, you work hard to make your dreams come true, taking pride in a job well done.

**Embrace:** Relaxation; a peaceful heart; temperance

**Avoid:** Inhibitions; restrictive measures; false hopes

**Also born on this day:** Saint Francis of Assisi; poet T. S. Eliot; composer George Gershwin; singer/actor Olivia Newton-John; fitness guru Jack LaLanne; physiologist Ivan Pavlov; tennis star Serena Williams

# September 27 • Libra

You see life as a battle to be won. You are determined, scrappy, and much more physically energetic than the average Libra. You live very much on the surface of things, never afraid to show your emotions. While you can seem a bit pugnacious at times, you never lose your sense of fairness.

**Embrace:** Versatility; fidelity; imagination

**Avoid:** Extreme frugality; dogmatism; mistrusting others

**Also born on this day:** American revolutionary Samuel Adams; basketball player/coach Steve Kerr; actor Gwyneth Paltrow; baseball star Mike Schmidt

# September 28 • Libra

You love being in the spotlight. You have an effusive, natural charm that you often use to achieve your aims in life. Artistic and sometimes eccentric, you have the ability to communicate fluently via the nonverbal method known universally as "body language."

Embrace: Talent; self-respect; devotion to duty

Avoid: Narcissism; a fickle heart; superficial love affairs

Also born on this day: Actors Brigitte Bardot, Peter Finch, and Marcello Mastroianni; comedian Janeane Garofalo; TV host Ed Sullivan

# September 29 • Libra

You are a deeply sensitive person who enjoys keeping secrets. You relate very well to others on a one-on-one basis but may have trouble getting along with them in a larger forum. You have the typical Libra charm, although you don't always possess the confidence to exhibit it.

**Embrace:** Pioneer spirit; communication; illuminating truths

**Avoid:** Superstition; negativity; cynicism

**Also born on this day:** Actor/singer Gene Autry; author Miguel de Cervantes; physicist Enrico Fermi; journalist Gwen Ifill

# September 30 • Libra

You appear to be emotionally detached and aloof, but your personality resembles a volcano under an iceberg. With all your good grooming and perfectionist tendencies, you seem to have it all together, but you are actually much more explosive than you appear. You are not as easy-going and accepting as most Libras—in fact, you can be headstrong. You have an incredible appetite for life. You work hard, play hard, and never stop striving. You are incredibly focused on achievement and are willing to put all else on hold while you are involved in a project that's important to you.

**Embrace:** Openness; a forgiving spirit; erudition

**Avoid:** Being overly critical; pretentiousness; rivalries

**Also born on this day:** Author Truman Capote; actors Marion Cotillard and Deborah Kerr; singer Johnny Mathis

# October 1 • Libra

People born on October 1 have a bold and uncompromising spirit and an ability to come back from hard times. Drawing upon this strength gives you great satisfaction because it allows you to demonstrate your true mettle to others. You enjoy being in the spotlight yet have far too much grace to appear egotistical or vain. You understand the need to build your future on the successes of the past. You seek harmony in all aspects of life and have an instinct for making the right decisions in both personal and professional matters.

**Embrace:** Thoroughness; acceptance; happy memories

**Avoid:** A domineering temperament; disapproval; petty people

**Also born on this day:** Musician/actor Julie Andrews; aviation pioneer William Boeing; U.S. president Jimmy Carter; actors Brie Larson and George Peppard; baseball player Mark McGwire

# October 2 • Libra

People born on October 2 have personality plus. You are extremely charming and attractive to others, and have a great capacity for learning. You identify with the finer things in life. You take real pride in your appearance and have a strong sense of style. Even though you may seem to be concerned with the more superficial aspects of life, you are actually devoted to friendship and other essentials. You are a sensitive type who doesn't like to be in an environment that is noisy, ugly, or in any way unpleasant. You have many artistic aspirations, though you may be shy about expressing them.

**Embrace:** Transfiguration; religiosity; values

**Avoid:** Destructive impulses; self-righteousness; rages

**Also born on this day:** Indian activist Mohandas Gandhi; novelist Graham Greene; photographer Annie Leibovitz; comedian Groucho Marx; singer/songwriter Sting

# October 3 • Libra

You have great poise and composure. You are able to withstand difficult times without complaint and can learn major life lessons without seeming to change in any noticeable way. You are charming, and although you have a very healthy ego, you're not vain. While you may show a hint of the typical Libra frivolity, you possess great self-sufficiency and are incredibly logical. Although you want to live the good life, you may not be willing to bend all your efforts to this aim, because you understand that in order to be completely happy you must give at least equal time to your personal life.

**Embrace:** New ideas; protocol; taking risks

**Avoid:** Worry; predictability; empty praise

**Also born on this day:** Historian George Bancroft; singers Chubby Checker and Gwen Stefani; author Gore Vidal; baseball star Dave Winfield

# October 4 • Libra

Although Libra rebels are rare, you fall into this category. Of course, in the tradition of your sign, you are well bred and polite, yet you're a rebel all the same. You have respect for tradition, yet you make it a point to question social mores, especially outdated ones.

**Embrace:** Passion; respectability; good advice

**Avoid:** Trends; lack of focus; gossip

**Also born on this day:** U.S. president Rutherford B. Hayes; actors Charlton Heston, Buster Keaton, and Susan Sarandon

# October 5 • Libra

You experience considerable conflict between your intellectual and spiritual goals. You value learning, yet you understand that it is experience that brings true wisdom. You pride yourself on your sense of social responsibility, yet you never allow your political ideology to get in the way of having a good time.

**Embrace:** Humor; a sense of the ridiculous; simplicity

**Avoid:** Fear of change; an argumentative attitude; disinterest

**Also born on this day:** Rocket pioneer Robert H. Goddard; hockey star Mario Lemieux; actor Kate Winslet

# October 6 • Libra

You are a dreamer with a great need to express your inner drive through imagination and creativity. You love fantasy and illusion and are less concerned with the reality of existence than with the essence of it. What appears to be true is much more interesting to you than what may actually be true.

**Embrace:** Reality; purposefulness; a plan of action

**Avoid:** Frittering away time; escapism; unwise love

**Also born on this day:** Civil rights activist Fannie Lou Hamer; anthropologist Thor Heyerdahl; inventor George Westinghouse

# October 7 • Libra

You need to come out of your emotionally protective shell in order to meet your real destiny. You have a strong philosophical bent, which you often express through humanitarian activities. You try to use whatever influence you possess to help others. Although your opinions are often extreme, you have the dedication and commitment necessary to make a difference. There is a dark side to you that may not be apparent to any but those closest to you. Because of your tendency to be moody on occasion, it's important for you to be involved in lighthearted, life-affirming activities.

**Embrace:** Patronage; relaxation; holistic healing

**Avoid:** External pressures; nervous tension; sexual excesses

**Also born on this day:** Comedian host Joy Behar; cellist Yo-Yo Ma; writer Anita Shreve; Archbishop Desmond Tutu

# October 8 • Libra

You are a level-headed type who cannot be swayed by personal flattery. You possess the usual Libra charm, and the power of your personality is felt by all who know you. Still, you don't trade on this talent. You believe in paying attention to detail. You are personally ambitious yet care more for relationships than any professional enterprise. An ability to balance both is one of your trademarks. You have the ability to achieve your goals without any showiness or ego; you have the patience to take each day as it comes.

**Embrace:** Serenity; honesty; an ability to share

**Avoid:** Greediness; restriction; love of power

**Also born on this day:** Actors Chevy Chase, Matt Damon, and Sigourney Weaver; musicians Bruno Mars and Johnny Ramone; writer R. L. Stine

# October 9 • Libra

You have the natural gift of making peace. You possess a strong love of beauty and truth. Your unique and singular life is spent in the search for truth and in understanding both the material and spiritual aspects of your world. You are controversial yet good-natured. Whether or not you want to hear the truth, you will always ask for it. You need to feel you are living life on your own terms. You will gladly throw off all the trappings of status in order to get to a point where nothing matters except your personal autonomy.

**Embrace:** Bold challenges; maturity; stability

**Avoid:** Impossible odds; making enemies; a foolish heart

**Also born on this day:** Musician John Lennon; filmmaker/artist Steve McQueen; golf champion Annika Sörenstam

# October 10 • Libra

You play by the rules. You have a good sense of self and care a great deal about your personal reputation. Although you possess a pleasant temperament and a charming disposition, you lack a certain level of humility. Yet true to your Libran nature, you are never gauche enough to show it. You have the ability to command respect from others. You do this by exerting your own brand of subtle charm in ways that are completely irresistible. You need to feel as if you are constantly moving forward in life, so you embrace change.

**Embrace:** Wise use of power; unselfish motives; spontaneity

**Avoid:** Hesitation; dishonesty; hopelessness

**Also born on this day:** Football player Brett Favre; actor Helen Hayes; pianist Thelonious Monk; singer David Lee Roth

# October 11 • Libra

You have the ability to put other people at ease. You have a sweet and sensitive nature, which in no way implies a lack of strength. In truth, you possess considerable grit and determination and are often drawn toward adventure despite being somewhat afraid of what it will bring.

**Embrace:** Charity; good conscience; belief in self

**Avoid:** Emotionalism; inner fears; living in the past

**Also born on this day:** Choreographer/director Jerome Robbins; First Lady Eleanor Roosevelt; football star Steve Young

# October 12 • Libra

There are few individuals who possess the sort of generous spirit that you display. You enjoy living large, and you enjoy the respect and patronage of others. You are high-spirited and fun-loving, always looking for ways to have a good time with your many friends.

**Embrace:** Financial restraint; an open mind; inner voice

**Avoid:** Conflict; struggle; intemperance

**Also born on this day:** Actor Hugh Jackman; musician Sam Moore; opera tenor Luciano Pavarotti; newscaster Chris Wallace

# October 13 • Libra

You have enormous inner strength. You may have a fragile or quiet exterior, yet underneath that reserve you are pragmatic and loaded with common sense. You have the potential to be idealistic, yet you do not want to be caught off-guard. You are a true romantic at heart.

**Embrace:** Balance; opportunity; justice

**Avoid:** Guile; inability to forgive; need to dominate others

**Also born on this day:** Comedian/actor Sacha Baron Cohen; figure skater Nancy Kerrigan; musician Paul Simon; British Prime Minister Margaret Thatcher

# October 14 • Libra

You incorporate the very best traits of Libra. You are intelligent, diplomatic, and concerned with the sort of image you project to others. You have a flair for expressing yourself, and you are a master of communication. Although you may appear lighthearted on the surface, you are extremely serious at your core. You are introspective but still manage to display a warm personality. You are a good friend who believes in sharing all the joys and problems of life with the people you love. Because you have natural leadership abilities, you are often in the position of giving advice.

**Embrace:** Tranquility; harmony; sense of mission

**Avoid:** Mistrust; depression; unhappy love matches

**Also born on this day:** U.S. president Dwight D. Eisenhower; actress Lillian Gish; fashion designer Ralph Lauren; basketball coach John Wooden

# October 15 • Libra

You are a pleasure-seeking, luxury-loving individual. These traits are generally assets, but there are times when they cause you to become your own worst enemy. You are always quick to apologize for your real or imagined misdeeds but, unfortunately, you go on living your life in a way that makes the recurrence of such actions not just possible but probable. Goodhearted but often misguided, you can get yourself in a real bind simply trying to be honest, only to discover that everybody else is playing by different rules. People born on this date become more goal-oriented as they learn to trust themselves.

**Embrace:** Independence; strength of character; practicality

**Avoid:** Pretense; social climbing; superficiality

**Also born on this day:** Chef Emeril Lagasse; filmmaker/actor Penny Marshall; philosopher Friedrich Nietzsche; novelist Mario Puzo

# October 16 • Libra

You are a peace-loving individual who nevertheless can meet tough challenges. You have an engaging, almost childlike, love of making spontaneous gestures. Further, you have the ability to judge others in a wise yet kindly way. You have a strong humanitarian streak and display a great deal of concern for the welfare of other people. Your sincerity and lack of pretense draw others to you easily. You have the ability to set specific goals for yourself without becoming obsessive. You have great organizational ability and know how to take a project one step at a time.

**Embrace:** People of substance; information; wise choices

**Avoid:** Shyness; unrealized dreams; lack of fulfillment

**Also born on this day:** Irish revolutionary Michael Collins; actors Angela Lansbury and Tim Robbins; musician John Mayer; tennis player Naomi Osaka; writer Oscar Wilde

# October 17 • Libra

Complex and complicated, you understand the need to suffer in order to obtain wisdom. You must follow a circuitous route to your destiny, forced to learn important life lessons along the way. These are generally related to your relationships with others but include a great deal of personal soul-searching as well. You are savvy enough to realize that no matter how hard you work you may not receive the acclaim or status you want. That rarely deters you, because you are more concerned with your own efforts than the results. You realize that success is an arbitrary term.

**Embrace:** Empathy; pure motives; fidelity

**Avoid:** Scandal; impulsive actions; carelessness

**Also born on this day:** Rapper Eminem; astronaut/doctor Mae Jemison; actor/animator Mike Judge; daredevil Evel Knievel; playwright Arthur Miller

# October 18 • Libra

You are dynamic, spirited, and energetic. Not as diplomatic as the average Libra, you refuse to sugarcoat your opinions. You are ambitious, even a little aggressive, but you wear it well. You are not afraid to display your confidence. You are a real self-starter who believes in taking control of your life.

**Embrace:** Accountability; commitment to causes; spirituality

**Avoid:** Recklessness; self-admiration; a quarrelsome nature

**Also born on this day:** Musician Chuck Berry; football player/coach Mike Ditka; tennis champion Martina Navratilova

# October 19 • Libra

You are broad-minded and find fulfillment through bringing together the worldly and the spiritual sides of your nature. You have strong yet flexible opinions on many subjects. You are curious about life, have a fierce love for learning, and have the ability to transcend your own limitations.

**Embrace:** Virtue; anticipation; strength to dream

**Avoid:** Preoccupation; dishonor; fickleness

**Also born on this day:** Actor Richard Dreyfus; boxer Evander Holyfield; novelist John Le Carré; musician Peter Tosh

# October 20 • Libra

You embody the yin-yang principle: Duality is your defining characteristic. Your attitudes, even your personality, may seem changeable, yet you are merely displaying both sides of your nature. In order to understand yourself, you must be willing to accept your dark as well as your positive side.

**Embrace:** Facts; tradition; persistence

**Avoid:** Illusion; arrogance; flamboyance

**Also born on this day:** Director Danny Boyle; politician Kamala Harris; actor Bela Lugosi; baseball star Mickey Mantle; architect Christopher Wren

# October 21 • Libra

Smart, sassy, even a little sarcastic, you know how to put your personality on display. You are bold and creative, and you need your own space and aren't afraid to claim it. You're fun-loving, a bit mischievous, and you don't mind breaking a few rules now and then, stirring things up so that others take notice. You demonstrate the antic demeanor of a typical Libra, but your sense of emotional loyalty is very real. You like to do things your own way and would rather fail at something than give up control of your destiny.

**Embrace:** Diplomacy; family ties; the truth

**Avoid:** Empty praise; superficiality; frivolous ambition

**Also born on this day:** Poet Samuel Taylor Coleridge; baseball pitcher Whitey Ford; actor Carrie Fisher; musician Dizzy Gillespie; TV personality Kim Kardashian; writer Ursula K. Le Guin; chemist Alfred Nobel; jurist/TV personality Judith Sheindlin

# October 22 • Libra

You combine personal charm with intelligence and talent. Although you shine effortlessly in the spotlight, you are a natural loner who draws strength from privacy. You want to make your mark on the world and may even feel that you are destined to do so. Although your expectations may strike others as being naive, you take in all the possibilities available to you and ask "why not?" With your optimism and enthusiasm, you don't put up any barriers to what you can accomplish in life. If you want something, you go after it with surprising tenacity.

**Embrace:** Balance; serenity; being in the moment

**Avoid:** Loss of inspiration; looking back; dependency on mate

**Also born on this day:** Photojournalist Robert Capa; actors Joan Fontaine and Jeff Goldblum; novelist Doris Lessing; composer Franz Liszt; baseball player Ichiro Suzuki

# SCORPIO

## October 23–November 21

Scorpio is the eighth sign of the astrological year and is known by its astrological symbol, the Scorpion. Scorpio individuals are enigmatic, strong-willed, and passionate. With Pluto as the ruling planet, people born under this sign are considered to be dynamic and extreme in their opinions.

**Element:** Water
**Planetary ruler:** Pluto
**Key characteristic:** Endurance
**Strengths:** Intense; powerful; transforming
**Challenges:** Jealous; domineering; violent

# October 23 • Scorpio

Individuals born on October 23 have the charismatic personality so often found in those whose birthday falls on the cusp between signs. You have a definite flair for putting yourself into situations where you will be noticed, but then you are just as likely to pull back, vexed, when too much attention is accorded to you. You think big. You are not interested in listening to the reasons why something cannot be done, only in how to turn that negative into a positive. You enjoy living at a high pitch and would rather be in chaos than boredom.

**Embrace:** Artistic fulfillment; finding your soul mate; a positive self-image

**Avoid:** Being overly secretive; going to extremes; self-fulfilling prophecies

**Also born on this day:** TV host Johnny Carson; filmmaker Ang Lee; soccer player Pelé; actors Emilia Clarke and Ryan Reynolds

# October 24 • Scorpio

You have great personal magnetism. In love with life, you possess a highly romantic and sensual nature that defines your personality. You are extremely talented as well as fiercely competitive. You have a haughty disposition but are actually much nicer than you appear. You may have difficulty deciding just what you want out of life. Your talents often make things easy for you. Still, you want to strive, fail, then begin again: Only through this complicated scenario do you feel as if you've earned your place in the sun. Making relationships work is a key goal, which may be why you so often travel a circuitous route to personal happiness.

**Embrace:** Experience; activity; subconscious will

**Avoid:** Carnality; extravagant behavior; hidden agendas

**Also born on this day:** Actors F. Murray Abraham and Kevin Kline; soccer player Wayne Rooney; musician Bill Wyman

# October 25 • Scorpio

For you, the past is never very far away. You compare each new experience to what you have known. You don't believe in doing anything the easy way. You know what you want out of life and are not afraid to take a few risks to claim it. You learn from your mistakes and can turn adversity into success. With your extremely sensitive and highly imaginative nature, dreams and illusions are as concrete to you as reality. There is a certain ageless quality about you. In youth you may seem far older than your years, while old age only seems to refine your unique qualities.

**Embrace:** Poignant memories; artistic expression; peace

**Avoid:** Sadness; regret; addiction

**Also born on this day:** Comedian/TV host Samantha Bee; singer Katy Perry; artist Pablo Picasso; actor Marion Ross

# October 26 • Scorpio

You are easy to love, yet hard to know. You value power and know how to use it, but you are more concerned with using it to help others rather than to glorify yourself. You are extremely self-disciplined. Personal honor means a great deal to you, and you are a fanatic about keeping your word. No one else in the world is more likely to keep a promise than you are. You are interested in wielding power, though usually from behind the scenes. You will go to great lengths to put your ideas out there for others to see.

**Embrace:** Cooperation; commitment to excellence; kindness

**Avoid:** Wallowing in grief; being stymied by regret; obsessiveness

**Also born on this day:** First Lady/U.S. Secretary of State Hillary Rodham Clinton; game show host Pat Sajak; singer Keith Urban

# October 27 • Scorpio

You are a complicated person who likes to walk the tightrope between excitement and high risk. You can be sensible; you can be a daredevil. There's so much contradiction in your behavior that it's difficult to know how you'll react from one moment to the next—and that's the way you like it.

**Embrace:** Intellect; balance; friendships

**Avoid:** Negativity; insecurity; being too demanding

**Also born on this day:** Comedian John Cleese; explorer James Cook; writer Sylvia Plath; U.S. president Theodore Roosevelt

# October 28 • Scorpio

You are strong-willed, precise, and dedicated to doing a good job. You can become very disgruntled with yourself if you can't live up to your own expectations—which are occasionally far too ambitious. You are tough on others and tougher on yourself. You will never compromise your ethics to get where you want to go.

**Embrace:** A generous spirit; knowledge; involvement

**Avoid:** Dictatorial attitudes; perfectionism; willfulness

**Also born on this day:** Software developer Bill Gates; singer Brad Paisley; actors Joaquin Phoenix and Julia Roberts; scientist Jonas Salk

# October 29 • Scorpio

You are quixotic and sprite-like, with a changeable nature and an exciting personality. You always seem to be observing, rather than taking part. You dislike being the center of attention, even though you have the ability to draw the spotlight to yourself. You are the ultimate secret-keeper.

**Embrace:** Emotional stability; a hopeful heart; high ideals

**Avoid:** Envy; blaming others; troublesome love affairs

**Also born on this day:** Comedian Fanny Brice; actors Richard Dreyfuss and Winona Ryder; artist/TV host Bob Ross

# October 30 • Scorpio

You seek knowledge in order to gain wisdom, and you have an adventuresome spirit that manifests itself in a great love of travel and distant cultures. Although not academically inclined, you think of yourself as a lifelong student. You are an innovator in the way you live life, understanding that in order to progress you must be part of new experiences. To trust instinct over intelligence can be a challenge for you, but it is generally a sound goal. Not only can you make friends with virtually anyone, you are able to build up the self-esteem of others.

**Embrace:** Self-discipline; aptitude; benevolence

**Avoid:** Pretense; ambivalence; insensitivity to others

**Also born on this day:** U.S. president John Adams; soccer star Diego Maradona; poet Ezra Pound; rock star Grace Slick; actor Henry Winkler

# October 31 • Scorpio

You are in search of truth and spiritual oneness. You are not a rebel, but a loner, and you have no need of validation from others. Although your personal life may be characterized by highs and lows, you have tremendous endurance and can always get past a disappointment or a setback. Your forthright attitude allows you to display your honesty without seeming brusque or harsh. You get along well with others but are careful about enforcing emotional boundaries. You have great spiritual potential and are continually striving to learn more about yourself.

**Embrace:** Realization; psychology; self-understanding

**Avoid:** Questioning existence; disorganization; promiscuity

**Also born on this day:** Actors John Candy, Dale Evans, and Michael Landon; filmmaker Peter Jackson; poet John Keats; journalist Dan Rather; painter Jan Vermeer

# November 1 • Scorpio

November Scorpios are far more intense than their late-October cousins, but those born on November 1 are somewhere in between. You have a restless, energetic spirit, yet you are far more people-oriented than many natives of your sign. You want your place in the sun and are constantly striving for success. Even when you meet with serious obstacles, you remain a survivor with big plans about how to turn things around. You look to your friends for inspiration and experience, and you never take friendship lightly.

**Embrace:** Creative ambitions; constancy; taking ownership

**Avoid:** Negativity; apprehension; disenchantment

**Also born on this day:** Apple CEO Tim Cook; actor Toni Collette; novelist Stephen Crane; music producer/composer David Foster; singer Lyle Lovett; baseball player Fernando Valenzuela

# November 2 • Scorpio

You are a stubborn individual with an incredible amount of emotional and spiritual stamina. Although you often seem quiet and somewhat introspective, you are a fighter who supports the status quo and expects it to support you. You are the king (or queen) of high drama. Every emotional scene in your life is like something out of an opera. You are not someone who enjoys being disagreed with; because of that, you often get your own way. You have high standards and want to do everything on your own.

**Embrace:** Fairness; good judgment; tenacity

**Avoid:** Dogmatic attitudes; hypocrisy; possessiveness

**Also born on this day:** French queen Marie Antoinette; U.S. presidents Warren G. Harding and James K. Polk; singer/songwriter k.d. lang; actors Burt Lancaster and David Schwimmer

# November 3 • Scorpio

You are sarcastic, inventive, and extremely precocious. Your attitude of wry amusement seems to say that you know a few secrets about life that other people can't guess. Although you enjoy the good things that come your way, you never quite believe that your good luck will hold.

**Embrace:** Deep feelings; vulnerability; faith

**Avoid:** Rivalries; a desire to rewrite the past; cynicism

**Also born on this day:** Actor Charles Bronson; baseball star Bob Feller; football player/activist Colin Kaepernick; magazine editor Anna Wintour

# November 4 • Scorpio

Your need to create controversy exerts its will in every aspect of your life. Quick-witted and talkative, you tell the truth without fearing its consequences. Eccentric, even bizarre, behavior is the norm for people born on this date. You are the real article and will not deviate from your own standards for any reason.

**Embrace:** Discretion; fair play; an intuitive nature

**Avoid:** Tedium; feeling blue; looking back

**Also born on this day:** Journalist Walter Cronkite; actors Matthew McConaughey and Doris Roberts; humorist Will Rogers

# November 5 • Scorpio

You have a love of things that can be proven by scientific fact. You are a natural researcher and student. You are constantly looking for answers, cultivating knowledge and wisdom in order to better understand yourself. You don't do anything halfway or recklessly. More than anything, you believe in being happy.

**Embrace:** Good fortune; solace; facts

**Avoid:** Questioning authority; materialism; sarcasm

**Also born on this day:** Singers Bryan Adams and Art Garfunkel; actors Vivien Leigh, Sam Rockwell, and Tilda Swinton; actor/singer Roy Rogers; basketball player Bill Walton

# November 6 • Scorpio

You are a passionate, romantic individual with the ability to communicate on many levels. Although relationships are the centerpiece of your life, you are nevertheless extremely self-sufficient. You may seem serious on the outside, but you know how to have a good time. You are a lover of luxury and enjoy having all the familiar creature comforts. When you feel blue, you tend to pamper yourself. Honesty is the key to your relationships—you work very hard to make all of your personal relationships happy and honest.

**Embrace:** Comprehension; ability to reason; fate

**Avoid:** Secretive behavior; overwork; worry

**Also born on this day:** Actors Ethan Hawke, Sally Field, and Emma Stone; singer/songwriter Glenn Frey; film director Mike Nichols

# November 7 • Scorpio

Very few people have the potential you possess. You have intelligence and spirituality in equal measure—a marvelous combination. Although you possess a strong sense of mission in life, you are also profoundly inner-directed, needing a lot of time to concentrate on your personal sense of fulfillment. You take your friendships seriously and will keep your word to a friend without fail. Being a mentor as well as a pal is second nature to you. You are dedicated to doing good in your life, and you know that for you, family must always come first.

**Embrace:** Fortitude; a pure heart; innocence

**Avoid:** Absolutism; conflict; misunderstandings

**Also born on this day:** Physicist Marie Curie; evangelist Billy Graham; singer/songwriter Joni Mitchell; documentarian Morgan Spurlock

# November 8 • Scorpio

You must walk your own path in life, even if it is a difficult one, and you will usually resist help at every turn. You prefer to give advice rather than take it. You have a quirky vision that—though it may not align strictly with reality—is definitely your own. If you are bold enough to divulge that vision to others, you can be handsomely rewarded. You are extremely secretive and have a hard time allowing other people to be an intimate part of your life. You have amazing patience and can withstand delays and disappointments like few other people.

**Embrace:** Destiny; spiritual love; one's true self

**Avoid:** Compulsive behavior; spitefulness; disrespect

**Also born on this day:** Journalist/activist Dorothy Day; novelist Margaret Mitchell; singer/songwriter Bonnie Raitt; chef/TV personality Gordon Ramsey

# November 9 • Scorpio

You are extremely adventurous, energetic, and always on the lookout for new and interesting experiences. You seem to be constantly in motion, continually involved in new tasks and challenges. You have a definite need to live life on your own terms. You are supremely curious about life and never stop investigating the world around you, and you don't mind making mistakes as long as you learn from them. You understand that you cannot have the sort of life you want without taking a few chances, so you're more than willing to work without the proverbial net.

**Embrace:** Adventure; learning; deep feelings

**Avoid:** Risks; a defensive attitude; pipe dreams

**Also born on this day:** Politician Spiro Agnew; actor Lou Ferrigno; actor/inventor Hedy Lamarr; astronomer Carl Sagan; singer Mary Travers

# November 10 • Scorpio

You have so much strength of will that when you put your mind to it there is nothing you cannot accomplish. You possess a keen intelligence and brilliant insights. You often have a hard time deciding on just which goals you wish to achieve—the spiritual ones or the material ones.

**Embrace:** Sagacity; purpose; generosity

**Avoid:** Frivolity; weakness; squandering talents

**Also born on this day:** Actors Richard Burton and Ellen Pompeo; writer Neil Gaiman; theologian Martin Luther; lyricist Tim Rice

# November 11 • Scorpio

You are one of the world's true mystics. Unable to live life on a strictly material level, you depend upon knowledge and experience to take you where you wish to go. You have marvelous creative powers, which you put to use in even the most ordinary circumstances and everyday events.

**Embrace:** Graceful words; positive thinking; the will to win

**Avoid:** Indulging inner fears; spending too much time on petty details; power trips

**Also born on this day:** Actors Leonardo DiCaprio and Demi Moore; General George S. Patton; novelist Kurt Vonnegut

# November 12 • Scorpio

You possess a dual nature and may be perceived as either a saint or a sinner. You are essentially a loner, yet you have a magnetic personality that forces others to take notice of you. You can use your appeal in a manipulative fashion, though if you do, you run the risk of alienating others.

**Embrace:** Enchantment; self-reliance; devotion

**Avoid:** Unkindness; selfish motives; vindictiveness

**Also born on this day:** Actors Ryan Gosling, Anne Hathaway, and Grace Kelly; activist Elizabeth Cady Stanton; singer/songwriter Neil Young

# November 13 • Scorpio

Thanks to your powerful conscience and strong desire for personal autonomy, you have the ability to go against the "crowd." Uniqueness is so important to you that you have been known to actually adjust your opinions to deliberately conflict with those of others! You have a natural dignity in the way you carry yourself. You are humorous, spontaneous, and often lucky. You see things from a quirky perspective. You know the level of your own talents, but no matter what you have to offer, you will resist if you cannot do things your way.

**Embrace:** Ethics; appreciation; desire

**Avoid:** Irreverence; ill will; stress

**Also born on this day:** Actor Whoopi Goldberg; TV host Jimmy Kimmel; producer/director Garry Marshall; baseball player/coach Buck O'Neil; author Robert Louis Stevenson

# November 14 • Scorpio

You are deeply introspective and refuse to conform to the worldly standards of success. You have a deep affinity for nature, and you are at your most spiritually fulfilled when communing with it. You regard yourself in an abstract, analytical way and often make objective judgments regarding your motives and inner drives. Because you are extremely sensitive, you may appear aloof, even snobbish. Your friends, however, know how kind and considerate you truly are. You strive to achieve a spiritual oneness with nature. This gives you the solace you need.

**Embrace:** Insights; spiritual truth; modesty

**Avoid:** Craftiness; immorality; unhappy heart

**Also born on this day:** England's Prince Charles; artist Claude Monet; journalist/satirist P. J. O'Rourke; U.S. Secretary of State Condoleezza Rice; activist Bryan Stevenson

# November 15 • Scorpio

You are a fun-loving individual who enjoys being the center of attention. Your outward high spirits are something of a departure from the usual brooding Scorpio demeanor. You have the same level of intensity, but with a lighter touch. You like to feel that you are free to do anything you want in life. If you feel tied down or restricted in any way, you simply cannot be happy. You always look to get the most out of your personal relationships, but even if these turn unsatisfactory, you are unlikely to give up on happiness.

**Embrace:** Self-control; work ethic; spiritual wholeness

**Avoid:** Hysteria; gossip; perfectionism

**Also born on this day:** Actor Ed Asner; singer/composer Petula Clark; artist Georgia O'Keeffe; Judge Joseph Wapner

# November 16 • Scorpio

You have the ability to transcend your everyday experiences, gaining wisdom through encounters with others. You may seem wise beyond your years, even as a child. You have a solemn, almost stern attitude that makes you appear humorless, yet you actually have a wonderful personality. You are quiet and self-effacing, and when you choose to display your less complicated side, you are extremely likable. You are always on a quest to get to the bottom of things. You want answers to everything. You understand the value of learning from problems and disappointments.

**Embrace:** Accomplishments; religious faith; good will

**Avoid:** Frustration; notoriety; revenge

**Also born on this day:** "Father of the Blues" W. C. Handy; jazz musician Diana Krall; actors Maggie Gyllenhaal and Burgess Meredith

# November 17 • Scorpio

You carry yourself with great personal dignity. You have the rare ability to read the hearts and intentions of others. Your great wisdom gives you a spiritual view of life; because of this you refuse to get caught up in the superficial aspects of life.

**Embrace:** Evaluation; principle; acceptance

**Avoid:** Subjectivity; resentments; false friends

**Also born on this day:** Actors Danny DeVito, Rock Hudson, and Rachel McAdams; TV producer Lorne Michaels; director Martin Scorsese; baseball pitcher Tom Seaver

# November 18 • Scorpio

You are vibrant and energetic, and you possess amazing determination and an unbeatable will. You have a need to put your personal stamp upon existence. Never satisfied with "the way things are," you seek to improve and even perfect yourself. You tend to try to control everything around you.

**Embrace:** Self-expression; perseverance; plenty

**Avoid:** Loss of faith; preoccupation with minor details; delays

**Also born on this day:** Novelist Margaret Atwood; astronaut Alan Shepard; activist Sojourner Truth; actor Owen Wilson

# November 19 • Scorpio

Self-controlled and taciturn, you are likely to keep your own counsel. You have a powerful, almost magnetic presence that makes you a good leader, yet you do not mix well with others. One of your greatest talents is the ability to make other people feel good about themselves.

**Embrace:** Talent; independence; resoluteness

**Avoid:** Scarcity mentality; blunt remarks; injustice

**Also born on this day:** U.S. president James Garfield; TV/radio host Larry King; fashion designer Calvin Klein; actors Adam Driver, Jodie Foster, Meg Ryan, and Gene Tierney

# November 20 • Scorpio

You are a complex and complicated person who can be truthful to the point of recklessness. You strive constantly for achievement, eager to prove that "good guys" finish first. Loyalty is practically a religion to you—you make the best friend and the worst enemy. You have great protective loyalty to those you love, but you are quick to turn against those who hurt you or those close to you. Although you dislike change, you are often instrumental in bringing it about in the lives of others.

**Embrace:** Moderation; self-love; priorities

**Avoid:** Showmanship; bragging; harsh judgments

**Also born on this day:** U.S. president Joe Biden; politician Robert F. Kennedy; comedian/actor Joel McHale; actor Estelle Parsons; newscaster Judy Woodruff

# November 21 • Scorpio

You are humorous and infinitely practical. Quite simply, you're interested in getting the job done and having a good time while doing it. You see yourself as a mover and a shaker. A strong belief in your own skills and the ability to see the big picture keep you actively involved in projects that would intimidate other, less confident people. You are loving and thoughtful and have a great desire to bring joy into the lives of others. You are a hard worker with the common sense to know what must be sacrificed for success.

**Embrace:** Details; compliance; actualization

**Avoid:** Hasty decisions; instability; pride

**Also born on this day:** Singer Björk; magazine editor Tina Brown; actor Goldie Hawn; baseball stars Ken Griffey Jr. and Stan Musial; philosopher/writer Voltaire

# SAGITTARIUS

## November 22–December 21

Sagittarius is the ninth sign of the astrological year and is known by its astrological symbol, the Archer. Sagittarian individuals are jovial, intelligent, and freedom-loving. With Jupiter as the ruling planet, people born under this sign are considered to be understanding and principled. They have an appetite for learning and travel.

**Element:** Fire
**Planetary ruler:** Jupiter
**Key characteristic:** Benevolence
**Strengths:** Optimism; generosity; foresight
**Challenges:** Intolerance; self-righteousness; ignoring details

# November 22 • Sagittarius

You are fun-loving, yet you have a serious side. You often put yourself on the line for the people you love and the causes you value. You have so much class that it's impossible for anyone to dislike you. November 22 people love to travel and often find their truest friendships with people from other cultures. You are a big dreamer, and you aren't likely to map out your goals. You like to go where the wind takes you. You know how to maximize your level of enjoyment in life, but you are wise enough to know that material achievements don't always equal success.

**Embrace:** Redemption; karma; strength

**Avoid:** Procrastination; nihilism; divisiveness

**Also born on this day:** Tennis stars Boris Becker and Billie Jean King; novelist George Eliot; actors Jamie Lee Curtis and Scarlett Johansson

# November 23 • Sagittarius

You have a strong conscience, though you enjoy flouting convention. You are able to size up people and situations with ease. You are an idealist about romantic love but can bounce back from heartbreak. You have enormous leadership potential. November 23 individuals are often excellent teachers, sports coaches, and motivational speakers. Because you possess an entrepreneurial spirit, you often profit from your own ideas. Accumulation of fortune is seldom your aim, but you often accomplish it when you simply follow your best instincts. You live in the moment and prefer not to pursue scenarios that promise complications with minimal enjoyment.

**Embrace:** Respect; obeying the rules; normalcy

**Avoid:** Ridicule of others; sarcasm; scattering energies

**Also born on this day:** Chef Rick Bayless; singer/actor Miley Cyrus; actor Boris Karloff; U.S. president Franklin Pierce; politician Chuck Schumer

# November 24 • Sagittarius

You have an exceptional level of intelligence, yet you don't need to be identified with it for purposes of ego. You have a need for many friends. You especially enjoy people who have your gift for conversation and ideas. Love is a romantic idyll for November 24 people. You often fall for someone who is your opposite, and thus force yourself to deal with thorny philosophical issues. Since you are often academically inclined, you may overlook natural artistic abilities that may have been relegated to the role of hobbies. November 24 people make excellent chefs, writers, and comedians.

**Embrace:** Consistency; seriousness; unselfish motives

**Avoid:** Escapism; impulsive behavior; self-doubt

**Also born on this day:** Actor Katherine Heigl; composer Scott Joplin; basketball star Oscar Robertson; U.S. president Zachary Taylor; artist Henri Toulouse-Lautrec

# November 25 • Sagittarius

Individuals born on this date are in a constant search to connect with others. Your spirituality affects all your major decisions. It's virtually impossible for you to look at things from an opportunistic point of view. Far from losing out on success by this method, you manage to attract good things into your life because of it. You have more followers than friends because even though you are quiet, your spiritual aura is very strong and leads others to depend upon you. Despite your spiritual leanings, November 25 people have a rare gift for making and handling money. You are incredibly generous.

**Embrace:** Diligence; dedication to duty; humanity

**Avoid:** Resting on laurels; egotism; shallowness

**Also born on this day:** Industrialist Andrew Carnegie; baseball star Joe DiMaggio; singer Amy Grant; actors Christina Applegate and Ricardo Montalbán

# November 26 • Sagittarius

You are achievement-oriented and like to do things your own way. You give the impression of being hotheaded and stubborn. This attitude doesn't come from ego, but rather from an innocent sort of self-confidence. You use practical means to bring about seemingly impractical goals. People born on this date are self-disciplined and centered. You have a great deal of emotional toughness and feel that only through hard work and difficulty can you truly regard yourself as being successful. November 26 individuals are often drawn to an academic life. Knowledge is the linchpin of your nature, and this path is followed by dedication. Your ultimate goal is wisdom.

**Embrace:** A joyful heart; rewards; adaptability

**Avoid:** Intolerance; pessimism; regrets

**Also born on this day:** Air conditioning engineer Willis Carrier; singer/actor Robert Goulet; cartoonist Charles Schulz; singer Tina Turner

# November 27 • Sagittarius

There are few more independent thinkers than those born on November 27. You enjoy controversy and are apt to seek out an eccentric lifestyle. Plus, you successfully sway others to your point of view. You inspire others with your explosive personal style. Your sense of humor makes you notorious for playing practical jokes. You have the self-discipline to approach most of your goals with precision and hard work. You have the emotional and physical endurance to labor for long periods at a time without allowing outside distractions to take away your focus.

**Embrace:** Due process; deliberation; encouragement

**Avoid:** Superficial friendships; conceit; overspending

**Also born on this day:** Author James Agee; film director Kathryn Bigelow; musician Jimi Hendrix; martial artist Bruce Lee

# November 28 • Sagittarius

It's often said that people born on November 28 are their own best friend as well as their own worst enemy. You certainly know how to break rules in order to gain attention. But you're also divinely creative, with the ability to inspire others. You have amazing bursts of creative energy, as well as periods during which you produce very little. Because you often struggle to make sense of your life, you rely upon trusted friends for insight. You have a large circle of friends who are relatively unknown to each other. November 28 people make unusual career choices and change careers often because of their many and varied interests.

**Embrace:** The inner path; serenity; focus

**Avoid:** Lack of commitment; banality; mistrust

**Also born on this day:** Poet William Blake; film director Alfonso Cuarón; actor Ed Harris; comedian/TV host Jon Stewart

# November 29 • Sagittarius

You must learn to tell yourself the truth in all things. Friends provide a mirror by which you decipher your own image. You are often unwilling to set firm goals for fear you'll be unable to achieve them. This attitude needs to be dispelled before any progress can be made. To boost confidence, it is good to seek out careers that give you opportunities to project your personality through the work you do. Although you may be reticent to enter a career in retail sales, real estate, or teaching, November 29 people score high in all these pursuits after their first taste of success.

**Embrace:** A self-nurturing attitude; calm; togetherness

**Avoid:** Chaos; discord; impossible goals

**Also born on this day:** Authors Louisa May Alcott and C. S. Lewis; actors Chadwick Boseman and Don Cheadle; filmmaker Joel Coen; sportscaster Vin Scully

# November 30 • Sagittarius

You have a razor-sharp wit and the personality of a stage star. Forging friendships is not easy because you are extremely competitive. Your personality inevitably attracts others, however. People born on November 30 have unequaled sales skills, though they often favor another line of work. Smart alternatives include comedy, education, law, advertising, or writing. You have incredible luck with money, but gambling can be a problem if you don't learn to resist the urge. You have so much talent and personal appeal that you may find your goals come a little too easily. Many people born on this date are underachievers for this very reason.

**Embrace:** Daring; values; self-expression

**Avoid:** Trendiness; conflict with authority; meddling

**Also born on this day:** Politician Shirley Chisholm; British Prime Minister Winston Churchill; radio/TV personality Dick Clark; singer Billy Idol; baseball player Iván Rodríguez; authors Mark Twain and Jonathan Swift

# December 1 • Sagittarius

You live life on your own terms, which generally means very few rules. You see yourself as a glamorous figure and may at times favor a somewhat superficial approach to love. It takes someone really special to get you to settle down. You enjoy being in the public eye. You are not the sort who can labor behind closed doors. Instead, you enjoy professions that enable you to make use of your sparkling personality. People born on this day find interesting careers in sales, advertising, or show business. Although you prefer spontaneity to setting goals, you do have a strong will and can achieve amazing things when you put your mind to it.

**Embrace:** Free will; credibility; self-control

**Avoid:** Self-promotion; the dark side; controlling others

**Also born on this day:** Singer/actor Bette Midler; comedian/actors Richard Pryor and Sarah Silverman; golfer Lee Trevino

# December 2 • Sagittarius

You are highly romantic and talented. Although you seem strong, you are quite vulnerable. You seldom show your wounds, however, putting a positive spin on all events. December 2 people believe that, with a little luck, any dream can come true. Few people display the loyalty and affection to friends that you do. You are capable of great insight, and for this reason your friends often come to you with confessions or questions. You love on an epic scale. There is never any doubt concerning your sincerity. You often place your career goals above everything else. This is sometimes your way of coping with disappointments in other areas.

**Embrace:** Drama; courage; commitment to excellence

**Avoid:** Rash choices; envy; a broken heart

**Also born on this day:** Opera diva Maria Callas; football player Aaron Rodgers; tennis player Monica Seles; pop star Britney Spears; designer Gianni Versace

# December 3 • Sagittarius

Your charm, good looks, and winning personality make you incredibly appealing. You enjoy living the good life, yet always manage to keep in touch with spiritual values. You have a will of iron and can stand up for yourself in adversity and controversy. Although known for having a well-developed ego, this does not detract from your tremendous likability. You thrive on the challenge of pursuing a love object but may quickly lose interest. You have a bit of trouble making an emotional commitment because you likely equate it with giving up personal freedom, your most prized possession. December 3 individuals make spectacular dancers and actors. You tend to see the big picture rather than small details.

**Embrace:** Experience; direction; thoughtfulness

**Avoid:** Frivolous romances; moodiness; belligerence

**Also born on this day:** Novelist Joseph Conrad; actor Julianne Moore; rocker Ozzy Osbourne; singer Andy Williams; figure skater Katarina Witt

# December 4 • Sagittarius

People born on this date are risk-takers who never play it safe. You never attempt to be part of the crowd. You enjoy being different, as your eccentric attitude makes clear. You are intense about your personal freedom and will go to great lengths to achieve it. You will sacrifice anything—even love—to make this a reality. December 4 individuals have a love of electronic gadgetry and often look for career options in communications, mathematics, or various scientific disciplines. You have a genius for taking advantage of the spontaneous twists of fate that come your way.

**Embrace:** Rules; structure; inner dialogue

**Avoid:** Bad choices; misrepresentation; becoming sidetracked

**Also born on this day:** Actors Jeff Bridges and Marisa Tomei; essayist/historian Thomas Carlyle; Native American leader Crazy Horse; rapper/producer Jay-Z; artist Wassily Kandinsky

# December 5 • Sagittarius

You are a dreamer *and* a doer. You have a strong personal vision that informs everything you do, and which may become the focus of your life. Your challenge is to stay true to your ideas without being intimidated by the negativity of those who don't possess your vision or ability. You have an incredible ability to accurately judge the taste of others. Because of this gift, you have the potential to put your entrepreneurial skills to great use by marketing your own product or idea. You have a great belief in your ability to maintain your focus as you work to achieve your goals.

**Embrace:** Authenticity; intensity; readiness

**Avoid:** Confusion; fear; daydreaming

**Also born on this day:** Writer Joan Didion; entrepreneur Walt Disney; filmmaker Otto Preminger; musician Little Richard; U.S. president Martin Van Buren

# December 6 • Sagittarius

You are a kind individual with a genuine love of people. You are a natural mediator. Your positive attitude and exquisite good manners make you nice to be around. You raise sociability to an artform. You are an old-fashioned romantic. If you suffer a broken love relationship, you need a significant period of time for healing. Talent for mediating makes December 6 individuals excellent lawyers, judges, and corporate executives. If you go into the education field, you have a great impact on students who might otherwise have little interest in schooling. You have a strong drive to help others.

**Embrace:** Platonic love; a creative spirit; celebration

**Avoid:** Predictability; manipulation; mistakes

**Also born on this day:** Filmmaker Judd Apatow; lyricist Ira Gershwin; actor Agnes Moorehead; comedian Steven Wright

# December 7 • Sagittarius

You have great wisdom, which allows you to perceive life on many levels. You don't so much choose friends as you are chosen as a friend by others. You have a natural ability to act as a counselor, and you often dispense advice. Although you have many talents, you gravitate toward work in the arts. Those born on December 7 make talented musicians, photographers, painters, and dancers. Because you feel strongly that to do something strictly for money is unethical, finances are a tricky factor in your life. Your idealism is laudable, but it needs to be tempered with a more practical attitude.

**Embrace:** Good intentions; direction; promises

**Avoid:** Artistic pretensions; self-glorification; denial

**Also born on this day:** Baseball player Johnny Bench; basketball legend Larry Bird; actor Ellen Burstyn; author Willa Cather; linguist/philosopher Noam Chomsky

# December 8 • Sagittarius

Though you are usually headstrong, you also have a docile side. Because you possess a fascinating personality, December 8 individuals have no lack of people wanting to get close to them. You use the force of your personality to further your aims at work and prefer career choices that put you in the public eye. You are a big spender who enjoys showing your generosity to loved ones. You like to gamble, and should take care to monitor your emotional attachment to this pastime. People born on this date have considerable integrity and will not compromise it for personal gain. To you, winning counts only when it's achieved fairly.

**Embrace:** Good advice; a nurturing spirit; prudence

**Avoid:** Destructive behavior; impatience; being flattered too easily

**Also born on this day:** Singer/actor Sammy Davis Jr.; musicians Jim Morrison and Sinéad O'Connor; Mary, Queen of Scots; inventor Eli Whitney

# December 9 • Sagittarius

Although you have a jovial temperament, you also possess an edgy, somewhat sarcastic attitude that often draws you into controversy. You enjoy surrounding yourself with a group of people that knows how to have a good time. You may remain single, usually for fear that any relationship will dissolve in boredom. December 9 natives enjoy careers that allow them to travel. They thrive in the hospitality business and make good teachers, tour guides, or language instructors. You can be irresponsible in the way you handle monthly bills. Still, your forgetfulness is one of your charms. You have the resilience to bounce back from failures. Your natural optimism plays a big part in your success.

**Embrace:** Dignity; sociability; meditation

**Avoid:** Safety risks; deceit; excessive sarcasm

**Also born on this day:** Football star Dick Butkus; actors Judi Dench, Kirk Douglas, and John Malkovich; computer scientist/Navy Admiral Grace Hopper

# December 10 • Sagittarius

Analytical yet creative, people born on this date believe in getting things done. You don't like complications and will opt out of any friendship when too much is expected of you. If a mate doesn't respect the boundaries you put up, you may lose interest. Your ability to react coolly under stress makes you perfect for high-pressure jobs. December 10 individuals excel as surgeons, first responders, and air traffic controllers. You pride yourself on being invincible, and will do whatever you must in order to keep that image intact.

**Embrace:** Sensation; good work habits; privacy

**Avoid:** Detours; negative vibes; disillusionment

**Also born on this day:** Actor/director Kenneth Branagh; poet Emily Dickinson; chef/restaurateur Bobby Flay; abolitionist William Lloyd Garrison

# December 11 • Sagittarius

Intellectually gifted, you have the ability to transform your world into something quite amazing. A strong emotional nature makes you more intense than many Sagittarians. People born on December 11 are likely to be extremely passionate about their political views, especially in matters that affect the environment. You are usually the center of attention within your group of friends. You need to believe in your ability to make the world a better place through your work. Personal goals often revolve around travel and learning. You are a lifelong student who never passes up an opportunity to expand your horizons.

**Embrace:** Ecology; redemption; satisfaction

**Avoid:** Dwelling on unhappy memories; contradictions; intimidation

**Also born on this day:** Actor Teri Garr; singer/actor/dancer Rita Moreno; writer Aleksandr Solzhenitsyn

# December 12 • Sagittarius

People born on this date are competitive in all aspects of life. No matter how much you accomplish, you inevitably feel bad about the opportunities that got away. In romantic matters, you show a great deal of sophistication. Since friends are sometimes lovers and lovers are always friends, you remain friends with all of your exes. Articulate and witty, December 12 individuals often choose to make their living with words. You are well suited to work in journalism, comedy, advertising, academia, and law. You do many good deeds throughout your lifetime, demonstrating your goal to help others.

**Embrace:** Ingenuity; change; foresight

**Avoid:** Defensive behavior; danger; scarcity

**Also born on this day:** Writer Gustave Flaubert; painter Edvard Munch; musician/actor Frank Sinatra; singer Dionne Warwick

# December 13 • Sagittarius

Eccentricity marks your personality. When it comes to leadership ability, you are second to none, though that sort of role seldom appeals to your antic sense of fun. Even though you love having people around, you aren't big on making close friends. You feel that familiarity often breeds contempt. You are totally honest in all your relationships. If you are unhappy, you simply say so and move on. You are the original entrepreneur whose ideas are so far ahead of your time you can't help but succeed or fail in spectacular ways. Your mind is in a constant state of flux, churning out amazing—and sometimes impossible—concepts.

**Embrace:** Make-believe; learning; maturity

**Avoid:** Sensationalism; imitation; superficiality

**Also born on this day:** Actors Steve Buscemi, Jamie Foxx, Christopher Plummer, and Dick Van Dyke; singer/songwriter Taylor Swift

# December 14 • Sagittarius

You have the ability to juggle a variety of tasks and responsibilities. While others may be bemoaning a potential problem, December 14 people have already worked it out and moved on. People born on this date never differentiate between a good friend, an old friend, or a best friend. Friends simply are, and friends are what life is all about. To be, to think, to do, to express—these are your goals. You have little interest in putting together a linear plan of life and achievement. If it feels good, if it helps someone, if it creates beauty for even an instant, you are all for it.

**Embrace:** Diversity; sentiment; enjoyment

**Avoid:** Stubbornness; lack of control; resistance

**Also born on this day:** Astronomer Tycho Brahe; actor Patty Duke; writer Shirley Jackson; politician Margaret Chase Smith

# December 15 • Sagittarius

You are success-oriented, but you have far too much integrity to ever go against your principles to get what you want. You constantly look to your pals for advice. Romance can be complicated for you, and you may endure more than your share of unrequited love. You never lose hope, though. You are often drawn to semi-public work. Retail sales is a particularly rewarding field for you, since it allows you to make use of your people-skills and charming personality. You have a strong work ethic and are delighted when rewards flow from your efforts. You seem destined to easily draw money into your life.

**Embrace:** Spiritual transcendence; facts; belief

**Avoid:** Mood swings; bad temper; tardiness

**Also born on this day:** Actor Rachel Brosnahan; comic actor/writer Tim Conway; engineer/architect Gustave Eiffel; industrialist J. Paul Getty; novelist Edna O'Brien

# December 16 • Sagittarius

You have such a disciplined nature that you can live on very little, as long as you have the opportunity to express your inner fire. You believe that success equals creative accomplishment, not money. You have so much wisdom that you may seem to be plugged in to some cosmic energy source that the rest of the world can't see. You have a habit of pushing people away, especially when you most need help. You listen to your intuition rather than to conventional wisdom. You have high expectations for your talent, yet are willing to allow it to develop at its own pace. You believe that true art cannot be forced.

**Embrace:** Composure; common sense; fortitude

**Avoid:** Reclusiveness; indulgence; feelings of superiority

**Also born on this day:** Novelist Jane Austen; composer Ludwig von Beethoven; cultural anthropologist Margaret Mead; journalist Lesley Stahl

# December 17 • Sagittarius

People born on this date are material realists. Although you constantly aim high, you have the maturity to accept failure as part of the bargain. Your talent for leadership usually shows itself early in life, often through dramatic circumstances. Like other Sagittarians, December 17 individuals possess an entrepreneurial spirit. You have both the vision and the practicality to succeed in a self-run business. Your ability is predicated upon a keen understanding of what the public wants. Your tireless research efforts back up your intuition. You are likely to do well in graphics, publishing, catering, or pet care.

**Embrace:** Impartiality; organization; social skills

**Avoid:** Destructive habits; poor judgment; ruthlessness

**Also born on this day:** Conductor Arthur Fiedler; novelist Ford Maddox Ford; Pope Francis; actors Milla Jovovich and Bill Pullman; boxer Manny Pacquiao; poet John Greenleaf Whittier

# December 18 • Sagittarius

You are an energetic go-getter, yet you are never aggressive or abrasive in your dealings with others. You have an open, generous nature and a sharp sense of humor. You want to wake up every day eager to go to work. If your career can't support that level of enthusiasm, you'll look for something that does. Although you don't equate making money with success, you are concerned with maintaining a good standard of living. You don't believe in putting limits on what you can achieve, but you don't expect anything to come to you without a lot of hard work.

**Embrace:** Prestige; determination; inner power

**Avoid:** Lethargy; indecisiveness; lack of commitment

**Also born on this day:** Singers Christina Aguilera and Billie Eilish; baseball player Ty Cobb; actors Katie Holmes and Brad Pitt; musician Keith Richards; filmmaker Steven Spielberg

# December 19 • Sagittarius

You walk an emotional tightrope, but are utterly fearless. You revel in taking chances but never do it without a good reason. You are likable and make friends effortlessly. You feel the need to contribute to society through your work or your ideals. A strong sense of commitment to personal goals marks people born on this day as certain success stories. Your talent may get you in the door, but it's your moxie that keeps you in the room. The more difficult the odds against you, the more likely it is that you will succeed. You are happiest when you can use your professional status in order to effect positive change.

**Embrace:** Willpower; solidarity; true happiness

**Avoid:** Insincerity; bias; disbelief

**Also born on this day:** Singer Edith Piaf; actors Jake Gyllenhaal, Ralph Richardson, and Cicely Tyson; football player Reggie White

# December 20 • Sagittarius

You may struggle to break free of the image others have of you. Once you learn to see yourself as independent of your background or current situation, your true self can emerge. You choose friends you would like to emulate. You have an old-fashioned view of romance and may seek to connect with individuals who favor your happily-ever-after mentality. You have a way of drawing resources into your life without even trying. December 20 natives often choose professions that pick up the tab for travel expenses. You are fascinated with the world around you and look for ways to bring new experiences into your life.

**Embrace:** Self-determination; strength; ego

**Avoid:** Needy people; fear of change; stifling your true self

**Also born on this day:** Musician Billy Bragg; writer Sandra Cisneros; industrialist Harvey Firestone; actor Jonah Hill; film director George Roy Hill; producer Dick Wolf

# December 21 • Sagittarius

December 21 people often lack self-confidence and need others to help them feel good about themselves. You bring a high level of enthusiasm to your work. You need to feel personally involved and able to make a difference in your world. You have a talent for making good investment choices and are well equipped to handle your own financial affairs. You have the ability to reach the very top of your field once you learn to have confidence in your own abilities. Enormously talented, you can nevertheless be hamstrung unless you appreciate your gifts. When you learn how not to be your own worst enemy, your goals are apt to materialize.

**Embrace:** Excitement; emotional fulfillment; blessings

**Avoid:** Depression; sense of loss; low self-esteem

**Also born on this day:** TV host Phil Donahue; tennis star Chris Evert; actors Jane Fonda and Samuel L. Jackson; Olympian Florence Griffith-Joyner; musician Frank Zappa

# CAPRICORN

## December 22–January 19

Capricorn is the tenth sign of the astrological year and is known by its astrological symbol, the Goat. Capricorn individuals are controlled, conscientious, and practical. With Saturn as the ruling planet, people born under this sign are self-disciplined and hard-working. They are highly efficient and dedicated to becoming a success.

**Element:** Earth
**Planetary ruler:** Saturn
**Key characteristic:** Ambition
**Strengths:** Discipline; patience; structure
**Challenges:** Inhibited; depressed; rigid

# December 22 • Capricorn

You hide great sensitivity under a shell of pretended indifference. Although your circle of friends is likely to be small, you derive a great deal of happiness from relationships. You desire to love deeply but are afraid of the pain a broken relationship can inflict. It's only when you learn to trust your instincts that you find the perfect mate. Those born on December 22 tend to have a reputation for being workaholics. This isn't negative unless you are working hard to avoid issues related to relationships. You are often shy about revealing your goals to anyone, preferring to keep them secret in case of failure.

**Embrace:** Hard work; intensity; truth

**Avoid:** Guilt; selfishness; low self-esteem

**Also born on this day:** Actor Ralph Fiennes; composer Giacomo Puccini; newscaster Diane Sawyer

# December 23 • Capricorn

You never blame your setbacks on anyone but yourself. If a goal becomes impossible to fulfill, you simply replot your course. Because of your good attitude and innate ability to motivate others, you make an excellent mentor. You are exceptionally verbal and often tell enjoyable stories or anecdotes. You make friends effortlessly. You are unlikely to reveal confidences or ask for advice, however. You value stability in life. You are very serious about your career ambitions. You work hard, learn quickly, and obey the rules. You spend a great deal of money on home decorating, with an eye for pieces that will increase in value as the years go on.

**Embrace:** Details; imagination; a personal agenda

**Avoid:** Stress; demoralization; indifference

**Also born on this day:** Football coach Jim Harbaugh; actor Susan Lucci; religious leader Joseph Smith; musician Eddie Vedder; entrepreneur Madam C. J. Walker

# December 24 • Capricorn

You are totally unafraid of being yourself at all times. You are different—and proud of it. You often have a secret agenda that you are unwilling to divulge to anyone, even your closest friends. You are an interesting combination of free-wheeling and conservative. You know that by alternating your methods, you're most likely to meet with success—and success is the goal of everyone born on December 24. For most, this has to do with business or career, but for others it can mean family life, personal power, or even a sense of spiritual enrichment. One way or the other, you hitch your dreams to a star.

**Embrace:** Authority; magnanimity; decision-making

**Avoid:** Irrationality; instability; self-destructive habits

**Also born on this day:** Director Lee Daniels; actor Ava Gardner; business magnate Howard Hughes; singer Ricky Martin; author Stephanie Meyer

# December 25 • Capricorn

You are drawn to life's mysteries. You have an ability to read other people and understand their inner motives deeply. In romantic relationships, there is always a sense of the transitory, as if you aren't quite sure if you want to make things permanent. You are drawn to professions that allow you to indulge your love of knowledge. December 25 individuals make excellent lawyers, academics, and medical researchers. You are most likely to reach your goals if you have an emotional as well as material reason to succeed. If you experience a setback regarding a cherished goal, you are likely to try again, even harder, to achieve it.

**Embrace:** Tranquility; desire; new beginnings

**Avoid:** Laziness; lack of preparation; impossible odds

**Also born on this day:** Nurse Clara Barton; singer Jimmy Buffet; actors Humphrey Bogart and Sissy Spacek; baseball player Rickey Henderson; writer Rod Serling

# December 26 • Capricorn

You possess a determined, exceptionally serious nature. The close friendships you form remain part of your life for years. Romantically, you usually have your heart set on a firm commitment, though you may fall in love with people who do not. You are a meticulous, intelligent individual. You may seek to work in a creative field, but in the role of business or corporate figure. Those born on December 26 make excellent agents, corporate lawyers, and accountants. Money is the center-piece in your life. This does not imply greediness, but rather a desire to see that all your family members and loved ones are secure.

**Embrace:** Inner vision; forgiveness; kindness

**Avoid:** Overconfidence; repression; an authoritarian attitude

**Also born on this day:** Writer/composer/TV personality Steve Allen; actors Kit Harrington and Jared Leto; novelist Henry Miller; baseball player Ozzie Smith

# December 27 • Capricorn

You elevate style to an art, yet you are remarkably practical and down to earth. You tend to choose friends who share your views and values. You are excellent at getting others to work to their highest potential. You are about as good as it gets when it comes to handling money. Getting to the top of your profession is a natural goal for people born on December 27. Yet even your ambition has a practical side. You know better than to ignore all other aspects of life. You feel that your existence is fulfilled only if you can experience the joys of family life.

**Embrace:** Selectivity; romance; belief in the future

**Avoid:** Foolishness; temptation; inattentiveness

**Also born on this day:** Actors John Amos, Timothée Chalamet, and Marlene Dietrich; astronomer Johannes Kepler; chemist Louis Pasteur; journalist Corrine "Cokie" Roberts

# December 28 • Capricorn

Self-possessed and intelligent, you have great social skills, including the ability to make anyone feel at home in any situation. You take great pride and enjoyment in performing everyday tasks, believing that it is through the minor, not major, events in life that character is both formed and tested. You have a generally happy outlook on life. You have a great capacity for friendship. You often choose careers that put you in the spotlight. You do well in positions of power. You have a modest yet earnest desire to do the very best you can. Your goals tend to be carefully mapped out and may involve many years of trial and error.

**Embrace:** Political correctness; sociability; terms

**Avoid:** Artificiality; people who are only looking for fun; betrayal

**Also born on this day:** Comic book artist Stan Lee; singer/songwriter John Legend; comedian Seth Meyers; actors Maggie Smith and Denzel Washington; U.S. president Woodrow Wilson

# December 29 • Capricorn

You tend to experience a great deal of emotional flux in your relationships. You sometimes "freeze out" even your closest friends at one time or another because of differences in opinion. An ability to bear down and get past the fear that every relationship will fail is vital to your emotional well-being. You have great creative talent and likely opt for a career in the arts. If you choose another line of work, you're likely to have hobbies that give you the chance to use your creative abilities. You may feel vulnerable about your financial situation, even if you make a good salary. This "scarcity mentality" can cause you to make a few foolish decisions about money until you learn to move beyond your fear.

**Embrace:** Belief; long-range plans; reality

**Avoid:** Sacrificial love; addiction; envy

**Also born on this day:** U.S. president Andrew Johnson; actors Ted Danson, Jude Law, Mary Tyler Moore, and John Voight

# December 30 • Capricorn

You like the good life and are willing to work hard to achieve it. You believe that no one can have too many friends, and you enjoy making the social rounds. You want a romantic partner who shares your philosophical and religious beliefs. You have great leadership ability. Because of this, and your love of people, you make a wonderful supervisor or boss. You aren't known for taking risks, but you will walk on the wild side if it means a chance to experience something marvelous that will bring you knowledge or pleasure. You have a genius for devising a balance between your personal and professional lives. This is important, because you aren't content to be unfulfilled in either.

**Embrace:** Risk-taking; adventure; preparation

**Avoid:** Preoccupation; self-indulgence; greed

**Also born on this day:** Basketball star LeBron James; singer Davy Jones; writer Rudyard Kipling; baseball pitcher Sandy Koufax; golfer Tiger Woods

# December 31 • Capricorn

You respond to the demands of your heart, not your head. Because of your emotional intensity, you experience a great deal of instability in your personal life. This can be a drawback to your maturation. Although you have an instinct to lead a stable, productive life, your emotions tend to keep you from making good progress. You put feeling loved and valued ahead of professional success. If you are able to conquer your personal insecurities, you can be very successful in your career. You have enormous creative talent, and if you have the opportunity to tap into it, you are able to express your true self.

**Embrace:** Receptiveness; fantasy; the creative muse

**Avoid:** Willfulness; flattery; ego issues

**Also born on this day:** Pretender to the British throne Bonnie Prince Charlie Stuart; singers John Denver and Donna Summer; gymnast Gabby Douglas; actors Anthony Hopkins and Ben Kingsley; artist Henri Matisse

# January 1 • Capricorn

You have a truly aristocratic nature regardless of background or family connections. You demonstrate good taste in all aspects of life and know how to exist well, even on limited resources. You expect a great deal of yourself and always strive to live up to your full potential. This attitude translates to a quest for personal excellence, which can be rewarding but also exhausting, since you tend to be a perfectionist. You possess strong powers of patience and endurance and understand that some goals take a long time to become reality.

**Embrace:** True happiness; your spiritual path; emotional creativity

**Avoid:** Being overly sensitive; emotional isolation; anxiety

**Also born on this day:** Politician Barry M. Goldwater; baseball player Hank Greenberg; FBI director J. Edgar Hoover; actor Frank Langella; American patriot Paul Revere; novelists E. M. Forster and J. D. Salinger

# January 2 • Capricorn

Secretive and quiet, you present a stern face to the world. This persona belies your actual nature, which is considerably more animated and joyous. A sense of being judged by others keeps you from revealing your sensitivity to all but your closest friends. You seek quality, not quantity, in friendships and tend to cultivate a small circle of close friends. A certain level of personal detachment allows you to behave as a spectator to your own actions, learning from each experience. You don't credit others for your success, but neither do you blame anyone for your failures. Don't let the possibility of failure keep you from pursuing your dreams.

**Embrace:** Enthusiasm; spontaneity; a sense of humor

**Avoid:** Melancholy; self-pity; being contemptuous of others

**Also born on this day:** Writer Isaac Asimov; televangelist Jim Bakker; actor Cuba Gooding Jr.; supermodel Christy Turlington

# January 3 • Capricorn

You are resourceful and able to draw good things into your life without exerting much effort. You have a streak of originality, which is always evident in your personality and your work. You are naturally acquisitive: Material objects are important to you, but only as an outward expression of how you feel about your circumstances and the world around you. You often have difficulty expressing your true feelings, even to those closest to you. Your aspirations are endless. After you achieve one goal, you turn your attention to another. You never set any limits on what you can do, and because of this you usually succeed!

**Embrace:** Openness; availability; distinction

**Avoid:** Cover-up; self-indulgence; distractions

**Also born on this day:** Actor/director Mel Gibson; hockey star Bobby Hull; film director Sergio Leone; climate activist Greta Thunberg; writer J. R. R. Tolkien

# January 4 • Capricorn

You possess a quirky, quicksilver personality. You are dedicated to acts of kindness on a personal level, acts of humanity on a public level. You are extremely issue-oriented and are not shy about expressing your opinions, even unpopular ones. You don't care what sort of message you send, as long as you speak the truth. You have a heartfelt sympathy for the unfortunate, and you feel it is your duty to draw attention to the plight of such people. Your primary desire is to experience life in all its variety. You want to see and do things that most people miss. You delight in the challenges and rewards that come to you unexpectedly. To you, achievement is a relative concept.

**Embrace:** Freedom; precision; gratitude

**Avoid:** Transgressions; irreverence; pessimism

**Also born on this day:** Inventor Louis Braille; historian Doris Kearns Goodwin; writer Jacob Grimm; football coach Don Shula

# January 5 • Capricorn

Because you are so mentally focused, it is important for you to find ways to express your inner energy. You have strong opinions and don't expect friends to always agree with you—in fact, you appreciate a rowdy debate now and then. You are fascinated by small details and large events—the whole pattern of human existence.

**Embrace:** Tenacity; friendliness; harmony

**Avoid:** Boredom; pressure; complaints

**Also born on this day:** Actors Bradley Cooper, Robert Duvall, Diane Keaton, and Jane Wyman; novelist Umberto Eco; politician Walter Mondale

# January 6 • Capricorn

Contrary to most Capricorn natives, you are totally uninhibited, socially and personally. You refuse to be bound by the rules of convention, though you have an innate sense of decorum that allows you to be rebellious in the most courteous way possible. You make your own rules, and you are quite charming.

**Embrace:** True love; opportunity; popularity

**Avoid:** Defenses; obsessions; intrigue

**Also born on this day:** Comic actor Rowan Atkinson; rocker Syd Barrett; golfer Nancy Lopez; actor Eddie Redmayne; writer Carl Sandburg; film director John Singleton

# January 7 • Capricorn

You have a sensitive, vulnerable quality that endears you to others. You have a strong spiritual nature as well as a social conscience, and you are often drawn into political activism or humanitarian concerns. You are likely to experience a conflict between your inner-life needs and your external responsibilities.

**Embrace:** Renewal; rapture; intuition

**Avoid:** Transient affections; impermanence; confusion

**Also born on this day:** Cartoonist Charles Addams; actor Nicolas Cage; journalist Katie Couric; U.S. president Millard Fillmore; auto racer Lewis Hamilton; singer/songwriter Kenny Loggins

# January 8 • Capricorn

You seek to balance worldly concerns with an expression of your own needs. Although you strive for a pragmatic approach to life, you have an extremely superstitious nature and it's important to you that you are in control of your own destiny. Although you are very gifted, you may be riddled with self-doubts and profound questions about the nature of your place in the universe. These problems are exacerbated by the fact that you have difficulty expressing your feelings through words. You are noted for your loyalty and generosity. While you may dream big dreams, your true goal is to understand your own motivations.

**Embrace:** Sensuality; dynamism; stamina

**Avoid:** Overindulgence; greed; self-pity

**Also born on this day:** Singer David Bowie; actor Cynthia Erivo; theoretical physicist Stephen Hawking; singer/actor Elvis Presley

# January 9 • Capricorn

You are an extraordinarily complicated person who may occasionally seem to be at war with yourself. Brilliant and philosophical, you often maintain a facade in order to appeal to others. You reach for the stars, striving for perfection on every level, eager to prove your worth. You are ambitious and hardworking, and you often are content to sacrifice personal happiness in order to achieve career desires. Despite your very private nature, you have a great need to attract public notice. When you transcend your shyness, you may experience your most ambitious and satisfying successes.

**Embrace:** Spiritual values; initiative; ethics

**Avoid:** Hypocrisy; extravagance; dishonesty

**Also born on this day:** Singer Joan Baez; author Simone de Beauvoir; musician Dave Matthews; Kate Middleton, Duchess of Cambridge; U.S. president Richard Nixon; rock star Jimmy Page

# January 10 • Capricorn

People born on January 10 have heightened perception and fiercely held likes and dislikes. You are strong-minded and deal with others in a direct and honest manner. You have no secret agenda: You are proud of your forthright approach to life and may even flaunt it at times. Your swaggering attitude attracts others. You have the ability to make others see things through your eyes, change opinions, and change lives. Although your approach to projects may be somewhat unorthodox, you can think and act on the fly. You always manage to get the job done and have a sense of urgency about everything you do.

**Embrace:** Good manners; peak performance; duty

**Avoid:** Antagonism; pretense; misdirection

**Also born on this day:** American patriot Ethan Allen; singers Pat Benatar and Rod Stewart; agricultural scientist George Washington Carver; boxer George Foreman; sculptor Barbara Hepworth; actors Paul Henreid and Sal Mineo

# January 11 • Capricorn

You possess great personal dignity. You are a lovable person, yet you tend to be inflexible where your religious or political philosophy is concerned. Attractive and personable, you are also brilliant—a fact you may hide if you feel it gives you more leverage. You have the ability to rise from seeming obscurity to achieve everything you desire. Your intractable determination is legend, and it is by far your most remarkable characteristic. You're unlikely to be swept off your feet, since practicality dominates most of your thoughts and decisions. You feel that struggle adds to your sense of accomplishment. You understand that some goals take a great deal of time to achieve, but you have tremendous patience.

**Embrace:** Inner strength; sharing; psychic healing

**Avoid:** Patronizing attitude; coldness; aloofness

**Also born on this day:** Singer/songwriter Mary J. Blige; musician Clarence Clemons; Founding Father Alexander Hamilton; psychologist/philosopher William James; suffragist Alice Paul

# January 12 • Capricorn

You enjoy giving the impression that you are far more adventuresome than you are. You possess a good sense of humor and the ability to transcend your own limitations. Bold, imaginative, and undisciplined, you have an intellectual sophistication that few people can appreciate, and you go to great lengths to prove your abilities.

**Embrace:** Bravery; trust; exuberance

**Avoid:** Self-delusion; riding the moral high horse; incompetence

**Also born on this day:** Actor Kirstie Alley; Amazon founder Jeff Bezos; hockey player/businessman Tim Horton; writer Jack London

# January 13 • Capricorn

Fearless, reckless, eager to meet all of life's challenges—you often lead a tumultuous existence. You have a good sense of humor and can see the funny side of even the most difficult situation. You learn from your own mistakes, and if you are unable to envision the possibility of failure, it's because you are stubborn as well as optimistic.

**Embrace:** Transcendence; intelligent choices; values

**Avoid:** Failure; tedium; short-sightedness

**Also born on this day:** Writer Horatio Alger; actors Orlando Bloom and Julia Louis-Dreyfus; TV producer Shonda Rhimes; dancer Gwen Verdon

# January 14 • Capricorn

Highly ambitious, you are happiest when you juggle a variety of responsibilities, though you have a sense of humor about your obsessiveness. Scholarly and verbal, you are able to recognize your own limitations. You set high standards for yourself, yet you know how to take delays and disappointments without losing your enthusiasm or sense of fun.

**Embrace:** An ability to apologize; good judgment; vigor

**Avoid:** Acrimony; an arrogant attitude; sanctimonious behavior

**Also born on this day:** Actor Faye Dunaway; musician Dave Grohl; novelist John dos Passos; theologian Albert Schweitzer; director Steven Soderbergh

# January 15 • Capricorn

Although you wear the mask of practicality with conviction, you have a complicated nature. You want to create a lasting legacy. You seek comfort at every level of existence and are equally concerned with maintaining the comfort of others. Physically, emotionally, and spiritually, you do what you can to make the world a better place. You gravitate toward good feelings, good works, and good intentions. While you enjoy living in the lap of luxury, you never lose sight of the intangible virtues that truly make life worth living. You tend to be a loner, but you possess a special magnetism that draws people to you effortlessly.

**Embrace:** Laughter; spiritual riches; reachable goals

**Avoid:** Feeling blue; secret agendas; possessiveness

**Also born on this day:** Football player Drew Brees; actors Lloyd Bridges, Charo, and Regina King; civil rights leader Dr. Martin Luther King Jr.; film director/actor Mario Van Peebles

# January 16 • Capricorn

Although you have the temperament of a loner, you love people. You have the capacity to indulge your materialistic needs without losing sight of the importance of spirituality in your life. Something of an enigma to all who know you, you have an inner intensity that fuels all your actions. You connect with others on many levels, and you want to be challenged, both emotionally and intellectually, by your friends. When you use your considerable imaginative power and creativity and set your sights upon achievement, you have the heart to stick with it. You enjoy spending money on beautiful things and you are very generous.

**Embrace:** High spirits; a joyful heart; good health

**Avoid:** Escapism; irrational behavior; detachment

**Also born on this day:** Dancer/choreographer Debbie Allen; film director John Carpenter; industrialist André Michelin; actor/songwriter/director Lin-Manuel Miranda; model Kate Moss; writer Susan Sontag

# January 17 • Capricorn

You grasp the strong correlation between mental and physical energy. You're devoted to the notion of "peak experience," which may or may not be physical in nature. You operate on a level of almost primal instinct, trusting your intuition far above intellect in almost every situation. You continually put yourself "out there" in order to prove your abilities.

**Embrace:** Noble motives; intensity; high ideals

**Avoid:** Vanity; negativity; adulation

**Also born on this day:** Boxer Muhammad Ali; Founding Father Benjamin Franklin; actors Jim Carrey, James Earl Jones, and Betty White

# January 18 • Capricorn

With you, the accent is always on personal charisma. You can charm just about anyone, and you have the potential to be extremely manipulative if you choose. In most instances you are forthright, and you seek to be honest in your emotional dealings with others. You crave excitement and variety in your life.

**Embrace:** Loyalty; fairness; tact

**Avoid:** Limitations; loneliness; struggle

**Also born on this day:** Actors Kevin Costner and Cary Grant; soccer manager Pep Guardiola; comedian Oliver Hardy; author A. A. Milne

# January 19 • Capricorn

You recognize the strong connection between conscious and unconscious thought, which come together in dreams and creativity. You have an excellent grasp of worldly and esoteric wisdom. You are eager for professional and personal success and are wise enough to look to valued friends and associates for assistance.

**Embrace:** Brilliance; musical ability; security

**Avoid:** Excesses; instability; divine madness

**Also born on this day:** Painter Paul Cézanne; singer/songwriters Janis Joplin and Dolly Parton; author/poet Edgar Allan Poe

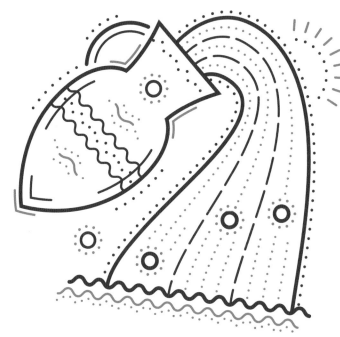

# AQUARIUS

## January 20–February 18

Aquarius is the eleventh sign of the astrological year and is known by its astrological symbol, the Water Bearer. Aquarius individuals are intelligent, progressive, and independent. With Uranus as the ruling planet, people born under this sign are considered to be free-thinking and unconventional. They will fight avidly for the rights of others.

Element: Air
Planetary ruler: Uranus
Key characteristic: Iconoclastic
Strengths: Humanitarian; modern; analytical
Challenges: Unreliable; extremist; chaotic

# January 20 • Aquarius

Individuals born on January 20 have a deeply personal vision of what their personal and professional lives are meant to be. You have a quiet determination that gets you through difficult times, and you tend to be concerned about the image you project. You make an excellent role model and are deeply committed to humanitarian causes. You are broad-minded about love and sexuality but have a certain cynicism about romance. You have a strong determination to succeed, and if you're able to follow your intuition, you can be amazingly successful. Few people learn more from their mistakes than you do.

**Embrace:** Versatility; curiosity; adventure

**Avoid:** Routine; defeatism; judgmental people

**Also born on this day:** Astronaut Buzz Aldrin; actor/comedian/singer George Burns; filmmakers Federico Fellini and David Lynch; comedian/political commentator Bill Maher; musician/producer Questlove

# January 21 • Aquarius

Cool on the outside, you possess a magnetism that puts you in the spotlight. Although you may appear somewhat egotistical, you are a generous soul. Sexual, spiritual, intelligent, and fun-loving, you can see the humor in things—even yourself. You are more conventional in romantic matters than many Aquarians. You may have some difficulty working for others—perfectionism is part of the problem. It's necessary for you to have many goals in order to keep you from becoming directionless. You need to understand that it is your own best efforts—not success—that crowns your achievement.

**Embrace:** Perspective; dedication; familiarity

**Avoid:** Danger; unpreparedness; surprise

**Also born on this day:** Actor Geena Davis; fashion designer Christian Dior; opera singer/conductor Plácido Domingo; golfer Jack Nicklaus; mystic Grigori Rasputin

# January 22 • Aquarius

You are talented and tend to call attention to yourself, enjoying being the focus of any group. Able to find the uniqueness in each experience, you enjoy the resonance of negative as well as positive emotions. You are typically attracted to glamorous types who mirror your own dark side. You may spend years developing your talents, and you always believe in yourself, even if few others do. When rewarded for hard work, you aren't content to revel in your good fortune. You set new standards for yourself, new heights to reach.

**Embrace:** A good reputation; discovery; popularity

**Avoid:** Lies; denial; self-neglect

**Also born on this day:** Ballet choreographer George Balanchine; gospel singer Sam Cooke; poet Lord Byron; actor Diane Lane

# January 23 • Aquarius

You are a hard-headed realist whose persona reflects a strong, silent type. There's a toughness about you that's at once laudable and useful: You seem able to handle anything. Inside, you're a tender soul. You hesitate to complain, and you hide your vulnerabilities for fear you'll be considered weak. Often put in the position of role model, you do not generally regard your conduct as anything special. You are motivated to achieve career success and may not realize until late that you also want personal stability. You want to be the best at what you do. You take criticism well and are able to look at yourself objectively.

**Embrace:** Humor; good luck; acceptance

**Avoid:** Solitude; antisocial attitudes; grudges

**Also born on this day:** American patriot John Hancock; actor Mariska Hargitay; painter Edouard Manet; pilot Chesley "Sully" Sullenberger

# January 24 • Aquarius

You feel a need to break patterns and shock those closest to you. Beneath the surface of your sophistication, you are kind and have a genuine love for others. You have the potential to do amazing things but may require the validation of others to believe in yourself.

**Embrace:** True self; dependability; thrift

**Avoid:** Making demands; physical excesses; risks

**Also born on this day:** Comedian John Belushi; singer Neil Diamond; gymnast Mary Lou Retton; ballerina Maria Tallchief; actor Sharon Tate; novelist Edith Wharton

# January 25 • Aquarius

You are cloaked in mystery, always holding something of yourself in reserve. Dreamy and introspective, you have intelligence, magnetism, and charm, as well as a profound sense of your own destiny. Commitment is not easy for you; you tend to idealize love. To make romance work, you need to come down to earth.

**Embrace:** Allegiance; growth; know-how

**Avoid:** Fair-weather friends; petty dislikes; crankiness

**Also born on this day:** Poet Robert Burns; singers Etta James and Alicia Keys; novelist Virginia Woolf

# January 26 • Aquarius

You make your own rules and are not afraid to strike out in unexpected directions. Your strength of character and steely intelligence give you a unique persona. Because you know the value of power, you are unlikely to misuse it. You thrive under pressure and need to prove what you're made of.

**Embrace:** Appeal; adoration; romance

**Avoid:** Unhappiness; unfocused energy; spite

**Also born on this day:** Comedian/TV host Ellen DeGeneres; hockey star Wayne Gretzky; U.S. General Douglas MacArthur; actor Paul Newman

# January 27 • Aquarius

People born on January 27 have excitable, magnetic personalities. You are alternately focused and indifferent. You may have trouble balancing the disparate sides of your nature, but this is one of your most intriguing traits. Your attractiveness has nothing to do with your looks. You have a taste for exotic romance and may have trouble being faithful, because although your heart is true, your spirit wanders. You can relate to individuals of all backgrounds and temperaments. Your talent for perceiving others' motives is extraordinary. Although not especially goal-oriented, you do set your sights on big dreams. Because you refuse to set limits, you have the potential to scale great heights.

**Embrace:** A sense of drama; power; graciousness

**Avoid:** Perplexity; hoping against hope; inertia

**Also born on this day:** Dancer Mikhail Baryshnikov; author Lewis Carroll; composer Wolfgang Amadeus Mozart; actors Rosamund Pike and Donna Reed; Supreme Court Justice John Roberts Jr.

# January 28 • Aquarius

You see yourself as a work in progress. You don't expect to assimilate all the experiences in your life overnight. While you strive for perfection, you realize it isn't a likely achievement. You have the common sense to be as tolerant and forgiving of your own faults as those of others. You are quite competitive, with an affinity for math, science, and music, and you have a talent for analytical reasoning. You aren't big on plans; you prefer to take life as it comes, no matter the consequences. You are curious about life, and that keeps you interested. You don't distinguish between professional and personal goals, knowing that in order to have a balanced life you need to concentrate on both.

**Embrace:** Honest mistakes; inner voice; attitude

**Avoid:** Fears; chaos; dictatorial behavior

**Also born on this day:** Actors Alan Alda and Elijah Wood; novelist Colette; painter Jackson Pollock; pianist Arthur Rubinstein; French president Nicolas Sarkozy

# January 29 • Aquarius

You are not content to watch the parade go by—you are spurred on by a powerful sense of mission. Although you may appear somewhat prickly to others, you are actually gentle and philosophical in nature, despite your strong political beliefs. You will put your reputation on the line to bring about necessary change. This need to do something for others isn't fueled by ego, but by conscience. You have a talent for inspiring and influencing others. You are often afraid of commitment because it represents to you loss of independence. You want to help others see the power and beauty of life. You love and respect knowledge and wish to share it with others.

**Embrace:** Ideals; distinction; irony

**Avoid:** Selfishness; controversy; destructive acts

**Also born on this day:** Writer Anton Chekhov; feminist Germaine Greer; U.S. president William McKinley; American patriot/essayist Thomas Paine; actor Tom Selleck; TV host Oprah Winfrey

# January 30 • Aquarius

You have an aristocratic bearing, yet are extremely accessible and friendly. You are generous and somewhat self-deprecating. It may be difficult for you to see your own good traits without having them validated by loved ones. You need your emotional space and will not sacrifice your independence. Even though you have natural leadership ability, you may seek out occupations that allow you to withdraw from the world. This isn't because you can't handle reality, but because you have too clear an understanding of it. Your goals are often too complicated for the average person to understand. You are so unconcerned with conventional goals that you may achieve great prominence because of your very indifference.

**Embrace:** Goals; good taste; fashionable appearance

**Avoid:** Lost opportunities; misjudging others; surliness

**Also born on this day:** Politician Dick Cheney; musician Phil Collins; actors Christian Bale, Olivia Colman, Gene Hackman, and Vanessa Redgrave; U.S. president Franklin D. Roosevelt; chess champion Boris Spassky

# January 31 • Aquarius

You have an eccentric perspective, with the charisma to charm just about anyone. You are intelligent and talented, but your brilliance can be undermined by foolish personal choices. Like many Aquarians, you have the ability to see beyond your concerns and look at life on a global level. You'll always find time to help others.

**Embrace:** Credibility; enjoyment; altruism

**Avoid:** Addiction; immaturity; silliness

**Also born on this day:** Actor Tallulah Bankhead; novelist Norman Mailer; baseball star Jackie Robinson; composer Franz Schubert; singer/songwriter Justin Timberlake

# February 1 • Aquarius

You are a rare breed: a rebel with respect for values. Something in your nature attracts danger. You can come too close to the dark side of your personality and must confront it. You want to show your independence in all things. You are unwilling to compromise your high standards in order to succeed.

**Embrace:** Exploration; confidence; leisure

**Avoid:** Superstition; losing interest; disappointment

**Also born on this day:** Film director John Ford; actor Clark Gable; poet Langston Hughes; musician Rick James; singer Harry Styles; Russian president Boris Yeltsin

# February 2 • Aquarius

You are a stickler for honesty. Liberty and self-determination are your chief goals. You will do anything and sacrifice anything so long as it provides autonomy. You don't see achievement as a linear path. You are more concerned with amassing life experiences that will help you reach your full potential.

**Embrace:** Good choices; lost causes; quietude

**Avoid:** Stifling your own creativity; bad habits; loose talk

**Also born on this day:** Model Christie Brinkley; actor Farah Fawcett; NFL great George "Papa Bear" Halas; novelists James Joyce and Ayn Rand; singer Shakira

# February 3 • Aquarius

People born on February 3 are talented, modest, and completely charming. You have the capacity to see both the big picture and life's small details. You can be eccentric, yet you may shelter yourself beneath a personality that reflects conventional views. You are devoted to family life. You put faith in careful planning, knowing that hard work pays off. You are an expert organizer who is eager to use your talents for humanitarian aims. You have a strong conscience, which balances your seemingly narcissistic side. People born on this day can focus on a project to the exclusion of everything else.

**Embrace:** Complex emotions; wonders of nature; happiness

**Avoid:** Emotional instability; pretense; self-interest

**Also born on this day:** Actors Isla Fisher and Nathan Lane; composer Felix Mendelssohn; illustrator Norman Rockwell; writer Gertrude Stein; football player Fran Tarkenton

# February 4 • Aquarius

You are intelligent and quirky. You can give the impression of being an "airhead," but in reality you are much more practical than you seem. You are inspired by what can be achieved through hard work. You have enormous self-discipline and can be extremely austere when it comes to cutting unnecessary encumbrances out of your life. Strong friendships are among your greatest joys in life. If only half of the goals you envision come true, you will consider yourself fortunate. You often tilt at windmills, yet your deep commitment makes it impossible for you to behave any other way.

**Embrace:** Being at ease with oneself; giving thanks; daring

**Avoid:** A critical demeanor; public opinion; cruelty

**Also born on this day:** Rocker Alice Cooper; feminist author Betty Friedan; aviator Charles Lindbergh; civil rights activist Rosa Parks; football player Lawrence Taylor

# February 5 • Aquarius

People born on this date have an intense and magnetic personality. Paradoxically, perhaps, you also have a loner mentality and keep to yourself, though you can shine socially. You are haughty yet lovable. You have a strict code of behavior and generally have equally strong religious or spiritual beliefs. You have a thoroughly modern outlook but are very set in your ways. You place less importance on your personal life than most people. Yet when you manage to find a relationship that works, you are spiritually and emotionally energized, and better able to handle all aspects of life without burying yourself in work.

**Embrace:** That special talent; mental energy; ecstasy

**Avoid:** Foolish risks; envy; codependency

**Also born on this day:** Baseball star Hank Aaron; writer William S. Burroughs; actors John Carradine and Laura Linney; soccer star Cristiano Ronaldo; politician Adlai Stevenson II

# February 6 • Aquarius

You possess a strong sense of personal integrity and the ability to act as a mediator. You embrace humanity and use your talents and personal goodness for the benefit of others. You have so much natural charm that even rivals compliment you. With a solid gift for friendship, you are eager to invite others into your circle. You have the potential for greatness, though you seldom realize this yourself. You are an ideologue and may find it difficult to reconcile your strong beliefs with the practical methods needed to make them reality. You have high ideals, and your primary goal is to uphold them.

**Embrace:** Ideals; honesty; spiritual harmony

**Avoid:** Capitulation; self-interest; wasting resources

**Also born on this day:** Newscaster Tom Brokaw; singer Natalie Cole; paleoanthropologist Mary Leakey; musician Bob Marley; U.S. president Ronald Reagan; rocker Axl Rose; baseball star Babe Ruth

# February 7 • Aquarius

You are a private person, but your great personal charm and sweetness make you popular. You need to make your ideas and opinions heard. This attitude affects every important act of life and comprises your spiritual and intellectual base. You don't pursue professional goals in a linear fashion, but are adventuresome, looking for life to provide some of the answers.

**Embrace:** Morality; truth; transcendental awareness

**Avoid:** Bitterness; emotional detachment; lies

**Also born on this day:** Singer/songwriter Garth Brooks; novelist Charles Dickens; basketball player Steve Nash; comedian Chris Rock; children's author Laura Ingalls Wilder

# February 8 • Aquarius

A certain spookiness is apparent in your personality. You have a powerful life-force with evidence of psychic awareness. Before you can use your talents and gifts, you must master—and understand—your personal power. You may have difficulty settling on a career. This is because you know that when you choose one road, you must give up exploration of another.

**Embrace:** Karmic lessons; sensitivity; spiritual harmony

**Avoid:** Carelessness; lack of focus; indifference

**Also born on this day:** Actors James Dean and Lana Turner; novelist John Grisham; TV journalist Ted Koppel; composer John Williams

# February 9 • Aquarius

You possess childlike innocence and great wisdom. You need to communicate your ideas through action. You accept struggles with grace, knowing you can only become what you envision through hard work. You follow your emotions, which, if not always wise, is honest. You get along wonderfully with others and work well in partnership. You aren't content to wait for things to happen; you rush headlong toward dreams.

**Embrace:** Belief; liberality; ethics

**Avoid:** Hostility; ill wishes; unpredictability

**Also born on this day:** Actors Mia Farrow, Michael B. Jordan, and Joe Pesci; singer/songwriter Carole King; novelist Alice Walker

# February 10 • Aquarius

People born on this date are high-energy types whose ambition for worldly success is grounded in motives other than materialism. You strongly believe in your abilities but are not egocentric. You fight for the underdog. Your ability to see beyond your own concerns is one praiseworthy characteristic. You have real concern and love for others, and are able to look at the total person without judgment. You are generous with your money, but not in a frivolous way. In your personal life, you seek to bridge the gap between the loneliness you may have experienced as a child and the sense of peace and contentment you seek in later life.

**Embrace:** Fellowship; self-determination; honesty

**Avoid:** Mediocrity; worry; irresponsibility

**Also born on this day:** Actors Elizabeth Banks, Laura Dern, and Robert Wagner; golfer Greg Norman; opera singer Leontyne Price; swimmer Mark Spitz; journalist/commentator George Stephanopoulos

# February 11 • Aquarius

You understand the powerful forces that can be commanded with discipline and training. You have a single-mindedness that allows you to sacrifice in order to bring a goal to fruition. Despite the seriousness of your commitment, you have a sunny side. You're able to balance the many different elements in your personal life without losing focus or emotional centeredness. Highly competitive by nature, you are determined to make it to the top of your profession. You'll go to great lengths and endure hardship to achieve your aims. You are all about commitment and find it hard to walk away from a challenge.

**Embrace:** Sensitivity; concern for others; emotional high

**Avoid:** Perfectionism; bad temper; exhaustion

**Also born on this day:** Actors Jennifer Aniston, Leslie Nielsen, and Burt Reynolds; singer/songwriter Sheryl Crow; inventor Thomas Edison; politicians Jeb Bush and Sarah Palin; novelist Sidney Sheldon

# February 12 • Aquarius

People born on February 12 have quiet strength. Your wisdom is based on karmic rather than worldly experience, yet you can live according to society's material constraints. You have the spiritual power to heal others' psychic wounds. Your Aquarian nature draws people to you, but you are a loner at heart and may have a difficult time making close friends. Smart use of your psychic awareness for practical applications in life is your chief goal. You are capable of doing spectacular things, but must first learn to assimilate the two sides of your personality. When you set your sights on a goal, you have the grit and determination to see it through.

**Embrace:** Positive attitude; confidence; destiny

**Avoid:** Negativity; disinterest; failure

**Also born on this day:** Writer Judy Blume; naturalist Charles Darwin; comedian Arsenio Hall; U.S. president Abraham Lincoln; basketball player Bill Russell

# February 13 • Aquarius

People born on this date are go-getters. Overcoming odds is what you live for, so you may invite a struggle when there's no need to do so! You have incredible energy, though you may not always use it wisely. You find it easy to get through life on your charm and good looks—but glitter is only one of your sides. Good-hearted and fun-loving, you don't expect a lot—only good companionship and an occasional shoulder to lean on. Your life goals may be unusual, but you can achieve them with determination and focus. You don't generally put all your ambition into career aims, preferring to indulge the personal side of life.

**Embrace:** Wise choices; moderation; faithfulness

**Avoid:** Inattention to detail; insincerity; gloating

**Also born on this day:** Singer Peter Gabriel; actor Kim Novak; TV host Jerry Springer; painter Grant Wood; pilot Chuck Yeager

# February 14 • Aquarius

High-strung and interesting, you possess an analytical intelligence that allows you to tackle complex problems without losing sight of the practical side issues. You have an edgy charm that makes you irresistible. Although you are not especially goal-oriented, you have a passion for pursuing your dreams. Your optimism makes you believe that anything worthwhile can—and eventually will—happen.

**Embrace:** Imagination; romance; sophistication

**Avoid:** Mental exhaustion; prejudice; false hope

**Also born on this day:** Comedian Jack Benny; journalist Carl Bernstein; NYC mayor Michael Bloomberg; abolitionist Frederick Douglass; broadcaster Hugh Downs

# February 15 • Aquarius

You exude sophistication and glamour, along with an aura of mystery and charm that impresses others. You are the picture of romanticism. Your sarcasm is usually reserved for extreme situations, but most of your loved ones feel its sting at one time or another. You would be best off learning to use your gifts to your full potential.

**Embrace:** Practicality; honest emotions; credibility

**Avoid:** Shallowness; frivolous emotion; excesses

**Also born on this day:** Suffragist Susan B. Anthony; actors John Barrymore and Jane Seymour; astronomer Galileo Galilei; cartoonist Matt Groening

# February 16 • Aquarius

Easygoing and generous, you give freely of your time and talents. You have a laid-back attitude that endears you to everyone; however, despite a pleasant facade, you are a perfectionist. When you involve yourself in a project, you give it everything. You are dedicated to getting maximum excitement out of life.

**Embrace:** Versatility; acceptance of change; mastery

**Avoid:** Quitting; discouragement; lost opportunities

**Also born on this day:** Actors Mahershala Ali and LeVar Burton; entertainer/politician Sonny Bono; tennis star John McEnroe; film director John Schlesinger

# February 17 • Aquarius

You are stable and intense, with strong views, yet you prefer to express yourself nonverbally. You are precocious emotionally and intellectually, and you occasionally fear the intensity of your feelings, so you make it a point to keep your emotions in check. You give the impression of being strong and capable, yet there are times when you feel on edge. You want to succeed even as you play by the rules. While financial security and career success are high on your list of goals, you are even more concerned with maintaining the meaning and integrity of your personal relationships. The superficial trappings of purely social relationships mean little to you.

**Embrace:** Self-satisfaction; dependability; practice

**Avoid:** Derision; dependence; losing faith

**Also born on this day:** Actors Joseph Gordon-Levitt, Hal Holbrook, and Rene Russo; basketball star Michael Jordan; comedian Larry the Cable Guy; singer/songwriter Ed Sheeran; businessman Thomas J. Watson

# February 18 • Aquarius

You are dedicated to the art of perfection and look at every goal as a personal challenge. You not only attract controversy—you thrive on it! Quiet and introspective, you have what it takes to become emotionally self-sufficient. When challenges come your way, you bear up stoically. You are tough on yourself, always looking to make each challenge more meaningful than the one that came before. You have good taste and like living well, but would never subvert your beliefs in order to make a good salary. Because of your strong humanitarian streak, you often bring a high level of political consciousness to your work.

**Embrace:** Wisdom; empathy; purpose

**Avoid:** Making demands; psychological strain; irritability

**Also born on this day:** Rapper/producer Dr. Dre; film director John Hughes; novelist Toni Morrison; artist/musician Yoko Ono; actors Molly Ringwald and John Travolta; TV personality Vanna White

# PISCES

## February 19–March 20

Pisces is the twelfth sign of the astrological year and is known by its astrological symbol, the Fish. Pisces natives are keenly in touch with their emotions, though never to the point of mawkishness. With Neptune as the ruling planet, people born under this sign are apt to be idealists who may do best when paired with a person who is by nature more pragmatic. Although Pisces individuals are physically and emotionally strong, they may put their hardiness to the test if they try to resolve the emotional conflicts of others.

**Element:** Water
**Planetary ruler:** Neptune
**Key characteristic:** Compassion
**Strengths:** Idealism; spirituality; transcendence
**Challenges:** Escapism; weakness; self-deception

# February 19 • Pisces

You have incredibly high ideals and are eager to learn, to discover. You are restless, eccentrically spiritual, and lean toward being emotionally fragile. At times, you are unable to assert your authority and thus have to struggle not to be managed by others. Governed by your emotions, you can sometimes be your own worst enemy. You are charming, kindhearted, and generous, but you tend to have a hard time feeling good about yourself; instead you rely on validation from friends and loved ones. You are devoted to your dreams. Because of your selfless nature, many of your dreams are for others.

**Embrace:** The joy of giving; ethics; leadership

**Avoid:** Predictability; censure; irresponsibility

**Also born on this day:** Astronomer Nicolas Copernicus; actors Jeff Daniels and Benicio Del Toro; singers Seal and Smokey Robinson; novelist Amy Tan

# February 20 • Pisces

People born on this date are deeply attuned to the spiritual mysteries of life. You possess a phenomenal memory. Your considerable intelligence—though considerable—is more of an esoteric understanding than an analytical skill. You have high ideals, though you aren't necessarily a practical creature. You combine a natural artistic ability with a deep spiritual understanding. Loneliness and lack of self-confidence often cause you to choose friends and romantic partners who are bad for you. It's important to learn how to set limits in your personal relationships. When you do, you'll be considerably calmer.

**Embrace:** A sense of wonder; perfection; emotional resonance

**Avoid:** Doubts; pretense; sleep disruption

**Also born on this day:** Photographer Ansel Adams; basketball player Charles Barkley; politician Mitch McConnell; comedian/TV host Trevor Noah; actor Sidney Poitier; singer Rihanna; fashion designer Gloria Vanderbilt

# February 21 • Pisces

You are acquisitive without being materialistic. Security-oriented, you seek social prestige but are generous with the resources available to you. People close to you know that they can always come to you for help without fear of being rebuked. Like most Pisceans, you are kind and giving, almost to a fault. You are generally fun-loving, yet you embrace responsibility wholeheartedly. Although highly motivated, you are not single-minded about success. To you, achievement means doing your best, without sacrificing other aspects of your life.

**Embrace:** Restraint; prudence; fiscal responsibility

**Avoid:** Intrigue; spendthrift habits; tension

**Also born on this day:** Writer Erma Bombeck; entertainment mogul David Geffen; fashion designer Hubert de Givenchy; civil rights leader/congressman John Lewis; comedian/film director Jordan Peele; actors Kelsey Grammer and Alan Rickman; singer Nina Simone

# February 22 • Pisces

You have a great deal of personal courage and are always ready to make tough decisions. Although extremely conscious of personal achievement, you are equally aware of the long and circuitous road you must take to get there. You often feel as if you are being directed more by fate than by your own will. More than anything else, you want to be allowed to live your life in a way you find pleasing. You are merely being true to your own instincts when you ignore the fast lane and choose to go through life at your own pace.

**Embrace:** Affection; lightheartedness; achievement

**Avoid:** Betrayal; confusion; disillusionment

**Also born on this day:** Actor Drew Barrymore; basketball player Julius Erving; poet Edna St. Vincent Millay; U.S. president George Washington

# February 23 • Pisces

You have the ability to reach emotional fulfillment on many levels and are not limited to the more orthodox understanding of spirituality that sustains others. You discover reality through a heightened sensitivity that can be difficult for all but those closest to you to understand. Because you are dedicated to helping others, it is sometimes hard for you to concentrate on your own concerns. People born on February 23 often gravitate to careers in the "caring" professions, and seldom, if ever, pursue a career path solely for financial gain.

**Embrace:** The strength to dream; creative inspiration; tolerance

**Avoid:** Self-pity; intolerant people; striking an attitude

**Also born on this day:** Writer/civil rights activist W. E. B. DuBois; actors Emily Blunt and Peter Fonda; film director Victor Fleming; composer George Frederick Handel

# February 24 • Pisces

You have a natural dynamism that sets you apart from other Pisceans. You are a go-getter who enjoys a varied and interesting social life. You may have difficulty finding a focus in your life, but when you do you are true to it. This often comes in the form of humanitarian concerns that provide you with just the sort of involvement you need in order to keep your life in balance. You may be confused about which direction you want to take in life, and you often benefit from the example of a friend or loved one who shows you the way.

**Embrace:** Trust; good intentions; faith

**Avoid:** Resistance; formality; pride

**Also born on this day:** Author Wilhelm Grimm; Apple co-founder Steve Jobs; composer/musician Michel Legrand; boxer Floyd Mayweather Jr.; actor Edward James Olmos; journalist Paula Zahn

# February 25 • Pisces

You are in tune with the world around you. You are ruled by instinct and intuition, yet you appreciate the value of an intellectual point of view, as well. When you learn to balance these two approaches, you find what you want in life. You have the potential to do great things, but you are even more powerful when you put your talents toward a cause greater than yourself. You understand yourself best through group involvement. You have an instinct for understanding and empathizing with the problems and concerns of others. Because your goals often change with your moods, you are on a constant search for new challenges and new horizons.

**Embrace:** Partnership; joy; living in the moment

**Avoid:** Instability; conceit; distractions

**Also born on this day:** Writer Anthony Burgess; musician George Harrison; actors Rashida Jones and Tea Leoni; artist Pierre August Renoir

# February 26 • Pisces

You see life on a large scale, yet your ability to perceive details is amazing. You're affectionate and gentle, and despite your strong ambition to succeed, you never lose sight of the importance of personal relationships. You extract the maximum from experience, never regretting an opportunity taken, even if it doesn't bring you the happiness you expected. You like to master your own fate. You have the discipline to work for others, but prefer not to, feeling that you cannot achieve your desired level of success unless you go your own way. You're extremely idealistic. You see no reason why your dreams can't be realized and are willing to sacrifice to make sure they are.

**Embrace:** Energy; perception; cooperation

**Avoid:** Egotism; unpredictability; anger

**Also born on this day:** Singer Johnny Cash; comedian Jackie Gleason; author Victor Hugo; fashion designer Levi Strauss

# February 27 • Pisces

You have great empathy for others. You are especially protective of those you love and will go to any lengths to secure their happiness. Your intelligence shows in the application of your intuitive talents. You are skilled at managing the lives of others and often take charge of situations outside of your circle. You have the ability to shine at almost anything you attempt, and you often turn your talents toward helping others. You are fearless when it comes to stating your opinions on the most controversial matters, and you have the power to effect great change and understanding.

**Embrace:** Good nutrition; practicality; wisdom

**Avoid:** Flightiness; insecurity; jealous rages

**Also born on this day:** Singers Marian Anderson and Josh Groban; ballerina Antoinette Sibley; novelist John Steinbeck; actor Elizabeth Taylor

# February 28 • Pisces

You strive for perfection and are tireless in your pursuit of excellence in all areas of life. You dream on such a lofty scale that your reach at times exceeds your grasp. You enjoy living in the limelight. You seek recognition, even if solely within your own circle. Although your own self-worth is not determined by the validation of others, you still gravitate toward it. You can transcend the difficult balancing act that causes so much trouble for so many people: finding enough time for personal and professional concerns without giving preference to either.

**Embrace:** Talent; sensitivity; distinction

**Avoid:** Excesses; no-win situations; enemies

**Also born on this day:** Auto racer Mario Andretti; architect Frank Gehry; economist Paul Krugman; hockey player Eric Lindros; film director Vincente Minnelli; actor Bernadette Peters

# February 29 • Pisces

Owing to your unusual birth date, you have unique talents and characteristics. You are good-natured, friendly, and almost unbelievably optimistic. You have a brilliant talent for seeing the positive side of any issue. While you are not naive, you do manage to retain a measure of your childhood innocence long after you entered the worldly phase of your life. Your youthful exuberance brightens your outlook no matter how bleak a situation may appear. Leap-year individuals insist on personal happiness. You have the ability to rise above any challenging situation and turn it into a success.

**Embrace:** Optimism; enthusiasm; happy days

**Avoid:** Trying too hard; childishness; making demands

**Also born on this day:** Motivational speaker Tony Robbins; hockey star Henri Richard; composer Gioachino Rossini; singer Dinah Shore

# March 1 • Pisces

You have strong views on morality, yet don't confuse them with deeper, spiritual truths. Your need to understand your own motivations is very strong. On many levels, it defines your character. You respect the status quo but rarely live your life in search of it. You are highly competitive and give your best at every opportunity, always believing that attitude, more than ability, promises success. Few people are more sentimental than those born on March 1. You extend this attitude to your family, with whom you likely experience a remarkable closeness throughout your lifetime.

**Embrace:** Celebration; improvement; discipline

**Avoid:** Charlatans; emotional instability; needless worry

**Also born on this day:** Singers Harry Belafonte and Justin Bieber; composer Frederic Chopin; film director/actor Ron Howard; bandleader/composer Glenn Miller; actor David Niven

# March 2 • Pisces

People born on March 2 have a perception that borders on genius. Although you may seem to clear everything through intellectual channels, you are really exercising your psychic sensitivity. Most of your major life decisions are made in this way. You are a gentle soul who may lack self-confidence. This is unfortunate, because you have many talents and can actually "find" yourself through judicious application of your abilities. You have a great need to display your intellect through practical means. You work very hard to make your dreams a reality.

**Embrace:** Self-worth; independence; meditation

**Avoid:** Insecure friends; dilemmas; scheming

**Also born on this day:** Actors Desi Arnaz and Daniel Craig; Russian statesman Mikhail Gorbachev; writer John Irving; singer/songwriter Chris Martin; baseball player/manager Mel Ott; children's author Dr. Seuss (Theodor Geisel)

# March 3 • Pisces

People born on this date tend to be fairly aggressive and opinionated. Professional goals are a definite priority, and success is an important goal in your life. But despite these attributes, you are also tuned-in to life's spiritual aspects and may be drawn to the supernatural. You approach life from a dreamer's perspective. In order for you to achieve your goals, you must accept challenges. This can be difficult, especially your struggle to overcome your loner mentality. You have a natural reluctance to ask others for help.

**Embrace:** Allure; great expectations; sympathy

**Avoid:** Passivity; fear of commitment; personal obsessions

**Also born on this day:** Inventor Alexander Graham Bell; actors Jessica Biel and Jean Harlow; fashion designer Perry Ellis; Olympic athlete Jackie Joyner-Kersee

# March 4 • Pisces

At times, life may seem to be a battlefield to the courageous and iconoclastic people born on this date. You seem to attract upheaval and chaos, creating a never-ending cycle of change. You hold yourself to a very rigid code of conduct, testing your character at every turn, and you have an all-or-nothing mentality. If you cannot reach the highest goals you have set for yourself, you may not be interested in attempting anything on a more modest scale. The challenge that awaits you is to work toward your lofty ambitions while also pursuing reachable goals.

**Embrace:** Mastery; self-knowledge; astrology

**Avoid:** Going to extremes; deliberation; blaming others

**Also born on this day:** Actors Patricia Heaton and Catherine O'Hara; football coach Knute Rockne; composer Antonio Vivaldi; singer/songwriter Bobby Womack

# March 5 • Pisces

People born on March 5 possess considerable intellectual courage. You are rarely afraid to take a stand or to own up to your controversial opinions. Even if you face stiff opposition to your ideas or plans, you will not allow dissent from others to sway you from your course. You are talkative and friendly, and you have a great talent for using words to your own benefit. You put a great price on the opportunity to share ideas and feelings with those close to you. You attract conflict and enjoy the chance to overcome it through your own efforts and hard work.

**Embrace:** Personal potential; perspective; wanderlust

**Avoid:** Ego issues; wildness; arguments

**Also born on this day:** Playwright Charles Fuller; actors Rex Harrison and Eva Mendes; magician Penn Jillette; composer Heitor Villa-Lobos

# March 6 • Pisces

You are a free spirit who refuses to conform to ordinary standards. You are not rebellious, since you respect structure, yet you choose to live outside it. One of the quiet Piscean types, you nevertheless communicate on a variety of levels. You are unafraid to take chances and would rather fail grandly than be too timid to try. You are unique in the extreme, and you celebrate your traits, not caring if your sometimes outrageous behavior earns the disapproval of others.

**Embrace:** Curiosity; true emotions; fellowship

**Avoid:** Snobbishness; empty promises; fatalism

**Also born on this day:** Poet Elizabeth Barrett Browning; economist Alan Greenspan; writer Gabriel García Márquez; artist Michelangelo; basketball player Shaquille O'Neal; Polish military leader Casimir Pulaski; actor/film director Rob Reiner

# March 7 • Pisces

March 7 individuals are among the most creative people and true visionaries. You are empathetic. Your sensitivity can transcend relationships of all types and definition. You have a profound need to experience life through the prism of your creativity. The insights you gain may not always be immediately recognizable, even to you, yet in time you come to know their value. You don't need to receive worldly rewards in order to feel your efforts have been crowned by success. Highly evolved in every way, you are accountable only to yourself.

**Embrace:** Integrity; inner beauty; spiritual fulfillment

**Avoid:** Rage; confusion; feelings of inferiority

**Also born on this day:** Baseball player Joe Carter; football player Franco Harris; actors Bryan Cranston, Jenna Fisher, and Rachel Weisz; composer Maurice Ravel; Scottish folk hero Rob Roy; comedian Wanda Sykes

# March 8 • Pisces

You are a fascinating combination of cynic and mystic. You may possess a loner mentality, yet you love people. You have a deep psychic consciousness, and you may prefer to spend your time pursuing humanitarian aims in a worldly forum. You are a puzzling and provocative person who, though you are able to see the very best in mankind, are deeply distrustful in your own personal relationships. You may reach adulthood undecided about the path you wish to take. Financial security is extremely important to you.

**Embrace:** Security; providence; gentility

**Avoid:** Fear; compromise; an unforgiving nature

**Also born on this day:** Dancer Cyd Charisse; Supreme Court Justice Oliver Wendell Holmes Jr.; singer/songwriter Shawn Mullins; actors Aidan Quinn, Lynn Redgrave, and James Van Der Beek

# March 9 • Pisces

You are devoted to the pursuit of excellence in all endeavors. You are extraordinarily sensitive at the core, yet are outwardly strong and determined. You are genuine and truthful. You have a great regard for spirituality in all its aspects and also possess a wicked sense of humor. You have very little regard for artifice and will freely speak out against it. You treasure your friends and allow them the sort of emotional intimacy most people reserve only for close mates and family members. You are constantly perusing your own character, searching for the one reality that will explore and explain the totality of your existence.

**Embrace:** Positive actions; goal-oriented achievement; dynamism

**Avoid:** Caution; pretense; superstition

**Also born on this day:** Actor Juliette Binoche; chess champion Bobby Fischer; cosmonaut Yuri Gagarin; writer Mickey Spillane

# March 10 • Pisces

You know how to draw the spotlight in any situation, and you usually manage to keep it on yourself for as long as you choose. Although you display a flirty, semiserious personality, there is considerable grit beneath the surface of your good humor. You can take care of yourself on just about any level and will never let anyone get the better of you. You have a great respect for learning and a reverence for wisdom, and you are dedicated to passing your knowledge onto others. You believe in working to positively affect the next generation.

**Embrace:** Courage; moral strength; sensuality

**Avoid:** Inflexibility; an implacable nature; coldness

**Also born on this day:** Composer Arthur Honegger; actor/martial artist Chuck Norris; actors Jon Hamm and Sharon Stone; singer Carrie Underwood

# March 11 • Pisces

You have the temperament of a true artisan. You are a gentle yet determined soul, and you follow a very personal path throughout life. You are drawn to extremes, and whether or not these have a positive effect, you will learn the lessons you need to learn. You are a stickler for truth and prize honesty. You are committed to finding inner peace. You have naturally pacifist tendencies, yet are quietly heroic. You want to succeed in life, yet are aware that success can be measured in many ways.

**Embrace:** Fascination; enchantment; mystery

**Avoid:** Distractions; pettiness; worry

**Also born on this day:** Civil rights activist Ralph Abernathy; writer Douglas Adams; singer Bobby McFerrin; media mogul Rupert Murdoch; bandleader Lawrence Welk

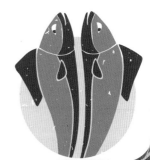

# March 12 • Pisces

You bring astonishing creativity and grace to everything you do. You are particularly adept at physical endeavors, but can also impart your natural artistry to important life interests. With so much artistic talent at your disposal, March 12 individuals are often drawn to creative professions. You possess a spiritually centered type of intelligence. You are incapable of acting from a strictly selfish perspective and are usually willing to sacrifice your own interests to accommodate those you love. You are fantasy-oriented, requiring periodic escapes from reality.

**Embrace:** Discipline; direction; preparedness

**Avoid:** Destructive impulses; confusion; guilt

**Also born on this day:** Playwright Edward Albee; writer Jack Kerouac; actor/singer Liza Minnelli; dancer Vaslav Nijinsky; politician Mitt Romney; singer/songwriter James Taylor

# March 13 • Pisces

Talented yet erratic, people with this birthday have a reputation for being high-strung. Your highly kinetic personality masks a temperament that finds it difficult to "go with the flow." Although generous by nature, at times, you may have trouble accommodating the views and needs of others. You have a strong sense of self and seldom question your own judgment. You never concern yourself with the reasons you cannot succeed at a goal, only why you can.

**Embrace:** Popularity; justice; normalcy

**Avoid:** Resentments; mistrust; meddling

**Also born on this day:** Business executive Jamie Dimon; actors Emile Hirsch and William H. Macy; singer/songwriter Neil Sedaka

# March 14 • Pisces

Prophetic and poetic, you combine intelligence with profound creative insight. You don't make friends easily, but once you do, it's for keeps. You must feel needed and indispensable or you cannot give of yourself to others. You have an artistic sensibility that is incredibly rewarding. Whatever you choose to do in life, that creative perspective will make itself felt. You rarely strive for success in any dollar-oriented way, yet you are likely to set personal goals that act as signposts on your journey through life.

**Embrace:** Realism; the life force; tenacity

**Avoid:** Naïveté; impulsiveness; the blues

**Also born on this day:** Gymnast Simone Biles; astronaut Frank Borman; actor Michael Caine; basketball player Stephen Curry; physicist Albert Einstein; composers Quincy Jones Jr. and Johann Strauss Sr.

# March 15 • Pisces

You are as straightforward as they come. You take things at face value and tend to be idealistic in all aspects of life, often refusing to address the questionable motives of others. Despite your intelligence, there is a certain naïveté about you, which endears you to others. You really cannot comprehend selfish behavior and are put off by negativity of any kind. You have very sincere friendships, and you put your emotional energy at the disposal of those you love. You wish to live a life that's simple and meaningful, honest and productive.

**Embrace:** Validity; compassion; fate

**Avoid:** Cynicism; emotional obsession; unreality

**Also born on this day:** Film director David Cronenberg; Supreme Court Justice Ruth Bader Ginsburg; actors Judd Hirsch and Eva Longoria; U.S. president Andrew Jackson

# March 16 • Pisces

You have a high-stakes attitude toward life. You are idealistic, yet have a wonderful capacity to understand and empathize with the struggles of others. You are a great cheerleader for your friends—you're unfailingly interested in their lives, and you do what you can to participate. It's important for you to find a harmonious balance between your career and personal life. You require a sense of security in your life. Learning to trust in the future can be a major breakthrough for you, as it eliminates the stresses that do so much damage to your peace of mind.

**Embrace:** Sensitivity; artistic integrity; miracles

**Avoid:** Compromise; being controlled; sexual excesses

**Also born on this day:** Film director Bernardo Bertolucci; actor Isabelle Huppert; comedian Jerry Lewis; U.S. president James Madison

# March 17 • Pisces

There is a hard edge of reality to you, even though you are warmly sensitive to your environment and day-to-day situations. You have the ability to set aside your creative endeavors and address practical problems when necessary. Nothing is a hurdle to you because you have an innate sense of what should take priority at any given time. Career goals are likely to be a major force through which all other aspirations are filtered. You are concerned with bringing together your dreamy side and your practical side. You vacillate between being an incurable romantic and a hard-boiled cynic.

**Embrace:** Objectivity; fun; appreciation

**Avoid:** Defensiveness; fatalism; wasting resources

**Also born on this day:** Singer Nat King Cole; golfer Bobby Jones; swimmer Katie Ledecky; actors Kurt Russell and Gary Sinise

# March 18 • Pisces

You depend upon your strong psychic awareness to guide your actions, and for this reason you may appear to be caught up in compulsive, even reckless, behavior. However, you are actually very centered, both emotionally and spiritually. You have a zest for life and are on a continual search for adventure. You are a pioneer who is never afraid to embrace personal and professional challenges. With a strong work ethic and limitless ambition, you are destined for career success. You have great organizational skills and will distinguish yourself in a career where your know-how can be accommodated.

**Embrace:** Values; laughter; premonitions

**Avoid:** Trade-offs; psychic pain; loss

**Also born on this day:** Speed skater Bonnie Blair; U.S. president Grover Cleveland; rapper/actor Queen Latifah; singer Wilson Pickett; writers George Plimpton and John Updike

# March 19 • Pisces

You are sensitive and possess a sunny disposition and a positive outlook. Although you can easily give yourself over to impulse and intuition, you understand the need to ground yourself in common sense. You are charming in a subtle, unassuming way. You instinctively understand your talents and weaknesses. You are often drawn to a career that allows you to conquer your inhibitions. Despite your trademark sensitivity, you are extremely goal-oriented and will sacrifice for years in order to make a cherished dream come true.

**Embrace:** Emotional healing; intellect; caring

**Avoid:** Restrictions; disparity; turbulence

**Also born on this day:** Actors Glenn Close and Bruce Willis; frontier lawman Wyatt Earp; novelist Philip Roth; Supreme Court Justice Earl Warren

# March 20 • Pisces

No matter how emotionally accessible you may seem, you always draw a veil between the persona you allow others to perceive and your real self. You are naturally drawn to the past, whether as a fount of your unconscious desires or the pool of your conflicted memories. To transcend barriers to reality is your way of bringing both worlds together, but is not a task that you choose to share with others. Learning to manage the sometimes wild impulses of your own creative psyche can be a major goal for you. You need to understand that breaking the rules simply to be different isn't the same as breaking those rules in order to do something worthwhile.

**Embrace:** Gracious living; high style; happy memories

**Avoid:** Controversy; regret; suspicion

**Also born on this day:** Playwright Henrik Ibsen; film director Spike Lee; hockey legend Bobby Orr; writer/actor/director Carl Reiner; children's TV host Fred Rogers